THE ORVIS

— GUIDE TO —

BEGINNING WINGSHOOTING

THE ORVIS® GUIDE TO

BEGINNING WINGSHOOTING

101 TIPS for the **Absolute Beginner**

Illustrations by
ROBERT L. PRINCE

Tom Deck

SKYHORSE PUBLISHING

Skyhorse Publishing books may be purchased in bulk at special discounts for sales promotion, corporate gifts, fund-raising, or educational purposes. Special editions can also be created to specifications.

For details, contact the Special Sales Department, Skyhorse Publishing, 307 West 36th Street, 11th Floor, New York, NY 10018
or
info@skyhorsepublishing.com.

Skyhorse® and Skyhorse Publishing® are registered trademarks of Skyhorse Publishing, Inc.®, a Delaware corporation.

www.skyhorsepublishing.com

10 9 8 7 6 5 4 3 2

Library of Congress Cataloging-in-Publication Data is available on file.

ISBN: 978-1-62087-619-0

Printed in China

*This book is dedicated to my son **J. Hudson Deck**.
No matter where your life takes you, I only hope that we will continue
to enjoy the outdoors together. You are by far the best hunting and fishing partner
I could ever have.*

Contents

Introduction

WINGSHOOTING IS AN EXCITING PASTIME WITH A RICH tradition. Every year, sportsmen take to the field in pursuit of their favorite game birds. The joys of wingshooting are frequently passed from one generation to the next. Hunters teach their children the rules, lessons, and techniques they have developed over many years spent afield. This passing of the torch includes long years of experience and dedication. One does not become an upland expert overnight, and even the best of bird hunters will admit that perfect days are rare.

Learning to shoot a shotgun can be an intimidating process if you don't know where to begin. My first tip is to find a mentor who has some experience in handling a shotgun. This can be a fun way to learn the basics, providing a go-to person who will take you to the shooting range or maybe even bird hunting for the first time.

Another option is to take shooting lessons or attend a shooting school. This can be the best way to learn some of the fundamental shooting techniques. Also, find and read books on shooting. This shouldn't be the only book you read on wingshooting and shotgunning. There are many wonderful titles you can read and explore. See Tip 96 for more information.

A few items to explain before you dive into this book. I use the words clay, target, and bird interchangeably. Also, most tips are written for the right-handed shooter. If you shoot left-handed (which I do), you will have to switch things around at times.

I have been very fortunate to have worked at the Orvis Fly Fishing and Wingshooting schools for almost twenty years. It has been my great pleasure to work with some very talented coaches. Much of this book comes from my experiences working with them. I have also been lucky enough to hunt and shoot in some wonderful places. The shotgun sports attract all kinds of people, and I've made many friends along the way.

I wish you all the best with all your shotgunning and upland adventures.

—Tom Deck
Manchester, Vermont
May 1, 2013

PART

I

Getting Started

1

Always make safety your first priority!

AS THE SAYING GOES, "SAFETY FIRST." IT ONLY SEEMS FITTING that our first tip cover safety and etiquette. I remember a hunting lodge I used to go to some years back that played an introductory safety video. One of the comments in it was, "You'll have a split second to react and a lifetime to remember." That line always stuck in my head. In the field, things can happen lightning fast, and it's important that the wingshooter always use good judgment and caution and be in control at all times. This is especially true when you are in the field with other hunters, and when dogs are on the ground.

The simple fact is that firearms can be dangerous, especially when used carelessly. But if you follow some simple rules, bird hunting will be less dangerous than driving your car to the shooting range or to your favorite covert.

Most states require hunters to take a hunter safety course before they can obtain a hunting license. This is a good place to start. You can easily find a listing of courses offered online. These cover the basics of firearms safety. However, it is important that new shooters receive hands-on instruction on how to load and safely handle a shotgun.

At the Orvis Shooting Schools, we have two simple rules that every shooter has to follow: *Never* point a gun at anything you don't intent to shoot, and treat every gun as if it were *loaded*, at least until you can verify that it is not. Another rule to follow that makes good sense is to keep the action open at all times when not shooting while continuing to treat the gun as if it were loaded. If it is an over-under or a side-by-side, break the gun open so its chambers are exposed. It is very comforting to other shooters to see a shotgun open or broken when you are not shooting. This is common shooting etiquette and good form, especially at shooting clubs where there tends to be a number of shooters gathered in close proximity.

Safety must always be at the forefront of the wingshooter. I once hosted a trip out West to a hunting lodge. We were hunting upland birds on the open prairie where there were very few trees. It was mostly rolling hills and a few river bottoms. I was matched up with a novice shooter who was very excited about his first bird hunt in Montana. The terrain was wide open, and I thought it would be perfectly suited for this gentleman's first hunt. It was just he and I, a guide, and his dogs.

The hunt started out wonderfully. We shot a few birds early in our hunt, and soon after lunch, we were approaching our limit. My partner was anxious to bag his limit of birds for the day. Pretty soon, the dogs locked up on point. Next thing we knew, a group of huns (Hungarian partridges) flushed out of the prairie. Birds were flying in all directions. In the midst of the action, a few of them flushed behind us. My partner, who had reloaded his gun quickly after the first rush of birds, was already swinging his barrels back behind us. I can still remember looking back over my shoulder as he swung his gun barrels directly across the chest of our guide. Our guide's face went white as he put up his hands and shouted, "Don't shoot!" It was a scary moment. Some ten years later, I can still see the look on our guide's face. Luckily, no one was hurt, but it was a lesson to all of us. No matter how open the cover and how safe it seems, you must always be in control of your gun barrels. Always put safety first, and always err on the side of caution.

Learn the rules and procedures for safely handling a shotgun.

2

Understand the difference the between a shotgun and a rifle

MANY NEW CLIENTS WHO COME TO AN ORVIS WINGSHOOT-ing School have had some basic introduction to firearms. More often than not, they were taught the basics with a BB gun or a .22 rifle. While this may be helpful initially, it's very important to understand that the rifle and shotgun are vastly different implements, especially in terms of ballistics and shooting technique.

I love a good Western, but Hollywood tends to romanticize the Old West. Movies often portray cowboys riding hard on a sun-baked western landscape shooting their rifles with deadly accuracy. Truthfully, many of the shots we see in the movies are next to impossible to pull off.

Let's begin with ballistics. A rifle shoots a single projectile, and a shot-gun shoots multiple projectiles. Think of your shotgun as shooting a swarm of smaller pellets toward the target. In a sense, you are trying to blanket— or cover—the target with a mass of pellets.

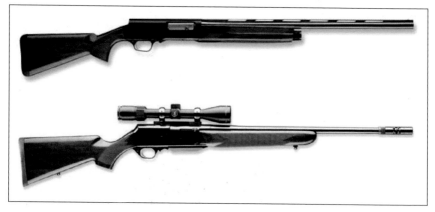

The shotgun shoots a swarm of pellets, often called a shot string. The rifle shoots a single projectile. (Photo courtesy of Browning)

The rifle is better suited for long-range targets that are stationary or moving slowly. The shotgun, due to its spread of smaller pellets, is better suited for close-range targets that are moving quickly. This swarm of pellets allows room for error when shooting at fast-flying targets such as upland birds or running rabbits. This margin of error is the main reason the bird hunter uses a shotgun to take small game.

Also, it's important to note that the techniques for shooting a rifle and shotgun are vastly different. A rifle bullet typically flies faster and farther than shotgun pellets. On a long-range target that is standing still, the shooter usually has time to take a solid rest and aim carefully.

A shotgun is best suited for targets that flush without warning and fly or run quickly away. There is certainly no time to rest the shotgun and aim at a bird rocketing through the air. When shooting moving targets, it's best to focus on the bird and simply point the barrel at the target. In the time it takes to aim at a fast-moving target, the opportunity will be lost. The successful wingshooter concentrates on the target, not his sights, and trusts that the spread of pellets will cover where his eyes are focused. There will be more detailed tips on shotgun shells, patterns, and techniques in later chapters, but it is important to understand the differences between the rifle and the shotgun.

3

Begin with a good foundation—take a lesson

THERE IS AN ELEMENT OF SATISFACTION DERIVED FROM blasting a clay target out of the sky. To see the clay bird explode against the canopy of fall colors is an experience that never gets dull. The wingshooter often begins the season by shooting clay targets to sharpen his technique. Some people simply enjoy clay target shooting and do not care to hunt game at all. Either way, the challenge of clay target shooting is truly exciting. Unfortunately, for someone just starting out, consistently hitting clay targets can be a challenge.

At first, the targets seem to be flying very quickly, and the shotgun feels heavy and clunky. Even the loud blast of the shotgun going off can be somewhat nerve-wracking to new shooters. Others may have a concern about recoil. How much is the gun going to kick when the shot is taken? All of these issues can easily be addressed before the new shooter steps up to the line for that first shot at a clay bird.

For those who are new to the game and don't have a mentor, the best option is to take a lesson or attend a shooting school.

In shooting, it's nearly impossible to see your own shot swarm flying through the air. This makes it difficult to make any adjustments in your shooting form because you don't really know where your shot string is going. This is where having a good instructor looking over your shoulder can really pay dividends.

As a professional shooting instructor, I'm biased on this subject. However, I've seen the benefits of shooting lessons firsthand. A novice who begins with a proper foundation has a real chance of becoming a fine shot in no time at all. Many times, a couple will attend a shooting school together. The wife will have little or no shooting experience, and the husband may have been shooting for years. It often turns out that the husband may have developed a few bad habits or has been shooting incorrectly for some time. The wife is a clean slate. No bad habits. No muscle memory programmed. Often with a little instruction, the new shooter quickly begins breaking clays. The experienced shooter often will struggle a bit, as the bad habits in his gun mount or ready position may take some time to correct.

It is said that it is easier to create new muscle memory from scratch than it is to break bad habits. In my years as a professional shooting instructor, I know this to be true. Often, bad habits are much harder to break if they are deeply rooted in the memory bank. Fixing a poor gun mount is much harder than learning it correctly the first time.

A typical shooting course is a two-day event. An organized shooting school typically has full-time instructors with experience and knowledge in proper shooting techniques. A school will cover many aspects of shooting and provide a good foundation for a person who has yet to pick up a shotgun for the first time. Many of our students at Orvis return each year for a tune-up for the upcoming bird season.

If you can't attend a school, find a local shooting instructor. Begin at a shooting club or range near you. If it's a quality shooting club, they will have instructors on site that provide lessons by the hour. Learning to shoot via a series of short sessions is a wonderful way to master the fundamentals.

A lesson from a professional instructor can be an excellent way to develop the proper shooting fundamentals.

Be sure to check your coach's experience level and affiliations. The best shooting coaches are often certified by some national organization or are affiliated with a reputable shooting company. Some instructors will specialize in clay shooting, and others may emphasize wingshooting technique. Also, experience matters: Coaches who have logged countless hours of instruction often have a better understanding of what it takes to help a new shooter progress.

Most instructors understand and promote proper shotgun fit. No matter which type of shooting you intend to do, it's critical that you learn with a shotgun that suits you. Gun fit is a vital component to proper shotgunning. It is extremely important that you learn to shoot with a shotgun that points where your eyes are focused. And, a shotgun must fit you before you can learn to shoot comfortably and accurately. An experienced shooting instructor should have a solid understanding of shotgun fit and how it benefits the shooter.

4

The over–under vs. the side-by-side?

THIS QUESTION HAS BEEN PONDERED FOR DECADES. BOOKS and magazines have pages full of text debating the merits of a side-by-side versus an over-under. Walk into any diner in South Dakota, Georgia, or Vermont on opening weekend of bird season, and there will be two fellows deliberating which gun is better.

Each style of gun has its own advantages and shortcomings. At the real heart of the matter is personal preference because both designs are effective for taking game or breaking clay targets. But there are pros and cons of each style that should be considered.

The purest wingshooter would certainly tell you that the side-by-side is the only gun the bird hunter should take afield. The modern gunner would most likely defend the over-under as the better sporting gun. There is no right or wrong answer on this one.

One issue to consider is the gun's intended use. Are you only going to shoot sporting clays, or are you going to bird hunt for grouse in the fall? Maybe a little bit of both?

The most obvious difference between the over-under and the side-by-side is the sighting plane. Look down the barrels of a side-by-side, and it's easy to see that it has a much wider sighting plane. An important fundamental of shotgunning is to focus on the target and not aim with the end of the gun. Having both barrels lying next to each other does create more mass at the end of the gun, which often proves distracting for some shooters.

However, some shooters are comfortable with the added mass and feel it's easier to point and swing a side-by-side.

The over-under has a single sighting plane. The barrels sit one on top of the other, so the sight line is much narrower at the end of the gun. The rib rests along the top barrel rather than in between the barrels of a side-by-side. The advantage of a single sighting plane is that it can be much less distracting because there is less mass at the end of the gun. Most clay target shooters tend to prefer a single sighting plane. This allows them to swing the barrels on line with the target without being distracted by the muzzle of the gun.

There are distinct differences between clay target shooting and bird hunting, but many wingshooters favor a side-by-side style gun. When hunting, birds can appear without warning and often fly unpredictably. A covey of quail can burst out of the brush like fireworks. The shooter often has mere seconds to react, and certainly there is no time to aim at the departing birds. In most upland situations, the wider sighting plane of a side-by-side really is not a distraction because the birds take to the air like miniature rockets. Bird hunting often makes you react to the flight of the bird. The hands and body must swing in concert with the flush of the bird. This instinctive reaction can be aided by the wider mass at the end of a side-by-side. Some shooters feel that the added mass helps them swing the barrels with the departing birds. Due to the quick reaction time and unpredictability of the bird's flight, there is little time to be distracted by the barrels of a side-by-side.

The clay target shooter often has much more time to set up and prepare for the shot. Typically, clay target shooters can often set the muzzle of the gun in the anticipated line of flight of the target. Often this spot is just below the sight line of the eyes. With the gun set in the ready position, the single sighting plane can be less distracting. Most clay target shooters tend to have a greater awareness of the concept of leading the bird. They tend to instinctively swing the barrels ahead of the target instead of aiming. The single sighting plane provided by an over-under affords them a clear picture of the clay without being a distraction.

Never underestimate the importance of shotgun fit. A side-by-side is much less forgiving when it comes to fit. It is certainly more difficult to connect with a side-by-side that does not fit the shooter precisely. Conversely, an over-under tends to be a more forgiving gun if it does not fit the shooter perfectly.

Side-by-sides tend to shoot a bit lower than over-unders. This is caused by a phenomenon termed "muzzle flip." When a side-by-side is fired, there is a minimal amount of flexure or downward thrusting that occurs. Often, a shooter will be fit with a straighter comb to compensate for this muzzle flip.

An over-under barrel configuration tends to stabilize the muzzles when fired. There is a more upward thrust as a reaction to recoil in an over-under.

The bottom line here is to be aware that each style of shotgun may fit you differently. In either case, make sure that the stock fits you precisely.

Side-by-side or over-under? Each type of gun has its merits, but it's really a matter of personal preference.

5

Don't overlook the semiautomatic shotgun

I'M NOT EMBARRASSED TO ADMIT IT. I AM A FIFTEEN-YEAR veteran of the Orvis Wingshooting Schools, I wear a tie to work, and yet I love a good autoloading shotgun. In fact, I have several in my own gun safe.

I'm well aware of the mystique of traditional hunting with double-barrel shotguns. I've hunted quail on horseback and shot sporting clays with a $100,000 side-by-side. I've even worn knickers and a tweed jacket while shooting driven birds. But for me nothing beats sitting in a duck blind with a trusty semiautomatic in my hands.

A semiautomatic shotgun offers the shooter a number of advantages. The most obvious is that it can hold two or more shotshells. That extra capacity can often make a difference when the air around you is full of ducks. (Although, keep in mind that it's illegal to have more than three shells in a shotgun when hunting waterfowl.) Also, there is measurably less recoil in most autoloaders. I taught my wife to shoot with a twenty-gauge autoloader, and she hardly noticed the recoil. For a new shooter, the perceived threat of recoil can become a real impediment. Many times, I'll be watching a student shoot, and they will actually close their eyes as they pull the trigger. This is simply a reaction to recoil. The body simply is trying to protect itself from the kick of the gun. This is often a subconscious reaction, and the shooters don't even know they are doing it. Put a dud shell in the gun, and they quickly realize they are closing their eyes, even flinching, as the trigger is being pulled.

I love to teach a shooter to use an autoloader. The semiautomatic shotgun can be a wonderful entry-level shotgun. The reduced recoil makes it easy to shoot time and time again, and I find most autoloaders to be very forgiving in terms of gun fit. Even if a semiautomatic shotgun doesn't fit a shooter perfectly, they still seem to be able to break targets with it. This is most likely due to the point of impact inherent in a single-barrel shotgun.

The side-by-side and the over-under barrel configurations are designed to overlap at approximately forty yards. This means that on a side-by-side gun, the right barrel shoots a little left and the left barrels shoots a little right at closer distances. The same holds true for an over-under. The top barrel shoots a touch low and the bottom barrel shoots slightly high until, at forty yards, they overlap each other. This may be ever so slight, but it tends to have an effect on the shooter, especially if the gun does not fit.

The single barrel on an autoloader does not have any compensation in the point of impact. The barrel tends to shoot in perfect alignment with the sighting plane of the rib. This creates a very accurate gun that has less recoil and is very forgiving to shoot.

Despite all these advantages, it's not all roses for the semiautomatic shotgun. For starters, it is harder to break down and clean than an over-under or a side-by-side. There are more moving parts that can cause trouble. Most break-action guns, like an over-under or side-by-side, tend to have three parts to clean. The autoloader, on the other hand, will have many more parts, and it can be difficult to reassemble once the parts are clean. Keep the owner's manual handy or have a gunsmith clean your autoloader for you.

The semiautomatic shotgun can be a joy to shoot.

Also, there is the question of reliability. Most autoloaders are gas-operated and tend to suffer from buildup over time. Once the action becomes gummed up, it may have trouble extracting or ejecting the spent shell. When this happens, the next shell won't cycle properly into the chamber, and the gun can't be fired until the action is cleared. The modern autoloader has become much more reliable and can shoot countless shells without a jam. Truthfully, the only time you have to worry about an auto jamming is when the gun has had some considerable use without proper cleaning or when you are using lighter loads. Lighter loads are shells designed mostly for target shooting. They have less powder in the shell and tend to produce less recoil, but the reduced charge may not be enough to operate the action.

There is also some etiquette to be followed when handling a semiautomatic shotgun. The break-action guns, such as an over-under, may be rendered safe simply by breaking the action open. At this point, the gun is inoperable and cannot fire. The semiauto cannot be opened in such a manner, so as a matter of etiquette, it's best to treat the auto as being loaded at all times. *Never* point the gun at anything you don't intend to shoot. When you are finished shooting, open the action and then carry the gun in a safe manner, so that others can see that the action is open, or put it in a secured rack. This is good form and allows others around you to see that the gun is not loaded.

Basic Shooting Techniques

6

Have the correct stance and footwork

A CORRECT STANCE IS THE FOUNDATION FOR ACCURATE shotgun shooting. How you place your feet does play a major role in how smoothly you can mount and swing your shotgun. Your stance sets up the body to accept the shotgun to the shoulder and cheek. The correct stance will also help to absorb recoil and aid your ability to track the target as it flies through the air. (I will be describing a right-handed shooter for this tip.)

A typical wingshooter's stance has the left foot pointing in the general direction of the target, with the right foot set back slightly, pointing at an angle of less than ninety degrees. It's easy to think about it in the context of a clock face. If the general direction you intend to shoot is twelve o'clock, then the left foot should be pointing at or slightly past twelve. The right foot should be set back a little for stability and point between two and three o'clock. Your stance can be adjusted slightly depending on your build or the type of shooting you are doing. A clay target shooter may have a more angled stance, and the wingshooter may prefer a squarer stance.

How you set up your feet in relation to the line of fire can vary slightly, but it's important to keep the upper body square to the target. This will insure that the upper body is free to mount and swing the gun.

The basic wingshooter's stance is somewhat narrow, with the heels somewhere between six and nine inches apart. How wide the stance is can depend on the build of the shooter. As a rule, the stance should be as narrow a possible without compromising balance. A stance that is too wide can inhibit the movement of the body on crossing targets.

The correct stance should set the upper body square to or just past ninety degrees to the direction of fire. This will insure that the shoulder pocket can receive the butt of the gun.

Compare this to the typical rifle shooter's stance and setup. A rifle shooter will have a much more angled stance, with the gun held across the body and chest. The shotgun shooter should be squarer in his setup and

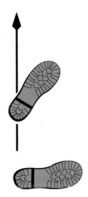

Angled rifle stance.

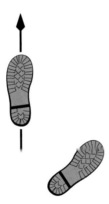

Traditional shotgun stance.

mount position. This helps because the butt of the gun needs to be held solidly in the shoulder pocket. If a shooter's stance is angled too much, the butt of the gun may end up on the upper bicep, inviting severe recoil bruising due to improper mounting of the shotgun.

Proper shotgun setup and stance should allow for a slight forward lean as the gun is mounted. The shooter's weight should shift onto the lead foot as the gun is lifted into the mounted position. It is much easier to lean into the shot with the lead foot pointing in the general direction you intend to shoot. This subtle forward lean helps the shooter absorb recoil and aids in mounting the gun without having to drop the head down to the stock.

The easiest fix to better shooting is the ready position

BIRD HUNTERS WHO COME TO THE ORVIS SHOOTING
Schools usually have a wonderful set of fundamentals. They mount the gun
with smooth confidence. They can track the bird with a keen focus and
break targets with reasonable success. However, the one thing that most
shooters don't have is a proper ready position. Luckily, this is a very easy
fix. Clay shooters are often amazed at how easily they can break even the
most difficult targets by developing a better ready position. Also, bird hunters always seem to have more time to swing onto the bird once they adopt
a correct setup.

When bird hunting, there is an appropriate way to walk through the
brush that keeps the shotgun muzzle pointed in a safe direction. The safe
hunting position has the gun held slightly across the chest. The butt of
the gun is held lower near waist level, and the barrels point up toward the
sky. The hunting position is an effective way to carry the gun safely while
watching the dogs work, but it is a lousy way to shoot. Think about it: If
the barrels are held high and you are attempting to shoot a ground-flushed
bird, you have to make a downward hatchet chop to connect with a rising
target. This is a difficult position to shoot from.

There is usually ample time to steady the gun into a ready position in
field situations. If you hunt upland game over pointing dogs, simply get the
gun ready when the dogs go on point. When working birds over flushing
dogs, it may be more difficult to maintain a ready position, but there is
invariably time to set up if you are alert and anticipating a flush. Most flushing dogs will become "birdy" when they get a snout full of scent. If you
pay attention to the dog's body language, you will know when the birds
are going to bust. Often, an experienced flushing dog will give signs that
are as reliable as a point. The nose typically drops closer to the ground and

the tail waggle becomes more intense. If you hunt behind the same dogs a number of times, it becomes obvious when they are going to put the bird up in the air.

The ready position is the starting point of the swing and gun mount. Once you have practiced it enough, the ready position will be a reliable and comfortable way to hold the gun prior to executing your move on the target. Begin with the barrels held just below the line of sight. This will afford you a clear view of the birds as you begin to track them in flight. You want to avoid having to look around or through the barrels to get a look at the bird. If you are shooting high birds on a driven hunt, the muzzle may be held high. When hunting upland game, the barrels will be positioned lower but still below the line of sight. Typically, the gun is held at an angle, so that the butt of the gun is tucked in below the armpit. The butt of the gun should not be held loosely below the elbow. Hold it so that it's snug to the body. If the stock is tucked slightly under the armpit, it forces the shooter to push the gun out to begin the swing and mount. This can help in pointing and swinging with the target as it takes flight.

Often, the easiest fix is to simply place the gun in a correct ready position prior to making your move on the target. The hunting position is a safe way to walk through a bird covert, but it can be a difficult way to connect with the target. Tucking the gun under the armpit and holding the muzzle just below the line of sight is the easiest way to improve your shooting technique.

The proper ready position has the stock held comfortably under the armpit and the barrels resting slightly below the line of sight.

8

Hands on the gun—point at the target for better shooting

SHOTGUNNING IS A SPORT OF MOVEMENT AND TIMING. THE finest shooters swing and mount the gun with a smooth elegance. As they swing the gun into action, they are pointing the barrels in concert with the bird, and the gun simply becomes an extension of their hands and eyes. Our natural pointing ability is the very foundation of an accurate swing and gun mount.

It's important to place your hands on the gun correctly when in the ready position. This helps you take advantage of your natural pointing ability.

Let's begin with the lead or left hand. The lead hand holds the forend and does most of the pointing and tracking of the target. Where should the lead hand be placed on the forend? Try this experiment: Point at a few clay targets with your lead hand without holding the gun. As you point and track the target, notice that your arm is fairly straight and extended. This is a natural way to point. So, the left hand should be extended as you draw the gun out of the ready position. Too often, I see shooters place the lead hand too far back on the forend. This creates an awkward bend in the elbow and makes it more difficult to point at a target in flight.

Why do shooters so often place the lead hand too far back on the forend? Most right-handed shooters rely too much on their right hand when they swing and mount the gun. Unfortunately, the right hand is not on the forend, it's on the grip. The right hand tends to overpower the left, and when this happens, the shooter does not properly engage the left hand. This often creates what is known as a "seesaw" mount. The right hand lifts the gun too aggressively to start the mount, and the barrel dips off the target line. The right hand dominates the move, and the lead hand tends to play catch up on the target. Those lost seconds often lead to a miss.

Each of the hands has a job to do. The right-handed shooter uses the left hand to control the direction of the barrel. The right hand raises the gun

Swing and point the gun at the target like you naturally would. This is often done with a nearly straight left arm.

up to the shoulder and cheek, finishing the gun mount. When each hand does its job, the gun stays on target, and the swing and mount is completed in a smooth, controlled way.

The pointing action of the left hand begins the gun mount. This will draw the gun out from under the armpit and place the barrels on the desired line of sight. The lead hand acts as an extension of the gun barrels.

If you are having trouble getting your lead hand started, extend your pointer finger so that it lies along the forend. It may even touch the barrels beyond the forend. By doing this you are instinctively pointing your finger at the target as you mount the gun. This can help the shooter with the swing of the gun with the lead hand, and it tends to make the shotgun move on the target with no seesawing effect to the barrels.

Use your lead hand to point at the target as you begin the swing and gun mount. This will promote a more efficient shooting style and lead to more success in the field.

Note that some shooters actually extend the pointer finger to enhance their pointing ability.

9

The gun mount—a steady head keeps you on target

"SHOULDER THE GUN!" YOU WILL HEAR THIS PHRASE A number of times during lessons, at shooting clubs, or at skeet ranges. It's one of the most misinterpreted tips in all of shotgunning. Aligning the butt, or back-end, of the stock to the shoulder is only part of mounting the gun properly. You must also line up the muzzle end of the gun with the eyes as you raise the gun up to the cheek.

What happens when the butt of the gun touches the shoulder pocket first? The head is often dropped down onto the stock to complete the mount. This minor head movement can make it difficult to focus on the bird. Excessive head movement accounts for many misses in the field or clay-bird shooting.

The correct gun mount is a smooth, steady process. The stock is raised up to the eyes and gently pressed into the cheek. This only makes sense because you are trying to line up the end of the gun with the eyes. The whole purpose of the gun mount is to make the gun point where the eyes are focused. A properly fitted shotgun should produce a consistent mount every time.

When the stock is placed properly against the cheek, the butt stock should align perfectly with the shoulder. The shoulder actually greets the butt of the gun as the stock is raised to the cheek. The goal is not to line the gun up with the shoulder. You are putting the gun up, so that it's pointing where the eyes are focused.

The correct mount has the shooter lifting the comb of the stock up to the cheek. The gun is then pressed into the cheek, so that a little flesh rolls over the comb. This provides a bit of a cushion and assures that the gun and eye are in alignment. This little cushion helps the shooter absorb the recoil without jarring the cheek bone.

Raise the gun up to the shoulder and cheek without dropping the head down to meet the stock. A steady head keeps the eyes on the target.

Get into the swing as you mount (timing and motion)

THE DOG HAS WORKED HARD AND SUDDENLY GETS BIRDY. Its tail begins beating back and forth, and then it locks up on point. In a nervous panic, the shooter brings the gun up to the cheek and shoulder. The birds burst from the brush on beating wings.

The shooter is unable to see the birds as they take flight. He lowers the gun from the shoulder to get a better view and then feverishly tries to recover, only to see the birds curving away in the distance.

What went wrong?

First, the shooter mounted the gun way too soon. The seasoned shot-gunner swings and mounts the gun in one smooth, harmonious movement. The swing and mount blend, and the shot is taken as the gun comes up to the shoulder and cheek. The novice shooter all too often mounts the gun up to the cheek and then tries to track the bird through the air, separating the mounting of the gun from the swinging action. If the shotgun is mounted too early, the receiver and the barrels may block the shooter's view of the target. This can make the bird seem as if it's flying much faster than it really is. The bird appears to be a blur screaming by the barrel.

It is much easier to track the target by swinging the muzzle onto the path of the bird and then mounting the gun with eyes fully locked onto the target. Avoid the temptation of shouldering the gun too soon. Instead, try to mount, swing, and shoot in one smooth motion.

A: Avoid lifting the gun to the shoulder and cheek and then chasing after the target.

B: The swing and gun mount should be one seamless motion. The stock should meet the shoulder and cheek only when the shooter is ready to fire.

The Eyes and Sight Picture

11

The dominant eye—if possible, shoot with both eyes open

WHEN YOU SEE A SHOOTER TAKE AIM WITH A RIFLE, HE closes one eye and aligns the sights down the barrel with the open eye. The shotgun shooter, however, does better if he shoots with both eyes open. Shooting with both eyes open can be a real advantage for the wingshooter. Why? When shooting with two eyes open, you are making maximum use of your natural binocular vision. This allows the shooter to track the angle and speed of the bird more accurately. Also, it is easier to determine distances more accurately when both eyes are open. Target acquisition and tracking will be much smoother if you use binocular vision.

If possible, shoot with both eyes open. Here the the gun lines up perfectly with the shooter's dominant right eye.

To shoot with both eyes open, you must establish which is your dominant eye. Also, your dominant eye must align with the shoulder you shoot from. Those who are strongly right-eye dominant and shoot right-handed can most likely shoot with both eyes open. I use the word "strongly" because there are varying degrees of eye dominance. Someone may shoot right handed and have a weak, but dominant, right eye. In some cases like this, the shooter's left eye may cause problems.

Here, the gun doesn't line up with either eye, and the shooter appears to have central vision.

To find out which which eye is dominant, try these simple tests: The first one I call the Circle Test. To begin, take your lead hand (the hand that holds the forend) and make an OK sign by touching the thumb and first finger. Then find something in the distance to focus on. Next, simply hold up your lead hand as if you were pointing the shotgun, and look through the circle with both eyes open. If you close each eye one at a time, you will find out which eye you are seeing the object with. For example, if you close your left eye and still see the object, you are right-eye dominant. Make sure that both eyes are open as you peer through the circle. This way, the dominant eye has a chance to take the lead and lock in on the object. Finally, close each eye to find out which is the dominant one. Do not close an eye and then lift up the hand and peer through the circle.

The circle test shows that this person is most likely right-eye dominant.

The pointer finger is lining up with the left eye. This suggests that the shooter is left-eye dominant.

The other test, which I actually prefer, is the Pointer Finger test. It is basically the same as the circle test except that you use the pointer finger on the lead hand. I will have students stand about twenty yards away and focus on my nose as they raise their hand and point at me. From there, I can clearly see which eye the pointer finger is lining up with. If the right pointer finger is directly lined up with the right eye, then they are clearly right-eye dominant.

However, sometimes this is not the case. Sometimes the pointer finger lines up with the opposite eye.

This is how the gun would line up on a shooter who is strongly cross-dominant.

When a shooter is right-handed, but has a left master eye, he is said to be cross-dominant. Some will have the pointer finger line up right in the middle of their eyes. This is known as central vision, in which case neither eye is dominant. It is probably better that such shooters do not keep both eyes open when pulling the trigger because the muzzle of the gun will, most of the time, line up with the dominant eye. So, if a shooter is cross-dominant and keeps both eyes open, the gun barrel will line up with the wrong eye. If the right-handed shooter is left-eye dominant and keeps both eyes open, the barrel will align with the left eye. Under these circumstances, the shot will miss significantly to the left.

This shooter appears to have central vision. No eye is showing dominance.

The remedy for these issues is the next tip.

Another test is to mount your gun and aim at a spot on the wall with both eyes open. Assuming that your gun fits correctly, you should be able to close the off eye and see if the gun is lined up with the object you are focusing on. If the tests indicate that your dominant eye consistently lines with the correct eye, then most likely you should be able to shoot with both eyes open. Again, remember that the gun barrel will want to line up with your dominant eye. If you shoot right-handed and your right eye is strongly dominant, they should line up perfectly, even when the left eye is kept open.

Binocular vision can really help the shotgunner lock onto the target. The speed, angle, and distance is best judged with both eyes open.

What can a shooter do if he can't shoot with both eyes open? There are some easy fixes, such as simply closing the off eye right before mounting the gun. However, be aware that whatever remedy is chosen, the shooter should acquire the target with both eyes open. This way the shooter can still use his binocular vision to track the flight of the bird. The next tip addresses fixes for the cross-dominant shooter.

12

If you can't keep both eyes open, wink at the bird

WHAT DO YOU DO IF YOU ARE CROSS-EYE DOMINANT OR your master eye doesn't completely line up with the gun barrel? The simplest solution is to wink the off eye at the moment the stock touches the cheek and then shoot. The simple closing action of the off eye will cause the open eye to align perfectly with the muzzle of the gun. The shot pattern will be on target and connect with where the eye is focused. Also, it's important to note that not everyone shoots their best with both eyes open. I know many deadly shooters who prefer to close the off eye when mounting the gun. Some are actually not cross dominant, but by closing the off eye, this seems to simplify the sight picture for them. It narrows their focus down to a single point. They simply wink the eye as the stock comes up while keeping their focus on the target. For many shooters, the sight picture can be too wide with both eyes open. Closing the off eye often narrows their focus and allows them to lock in on the target.

A quick wink as the gun is fired can become second nature with a little practice. Often, this can be done at home. Practice mounting the gun and closing the eye as the stock nears the shoulder and cheek. With some repetition, it will become second nature. Be sure to pick a target and focus on it as you wink the eye. Do not focus on the gun barrel during this practice drill. I always caution students to make sure they avoid focusing on the barrel as they continuously practice mounting the gun. If you lock in on the bead every time, you can be training yourself to aim with the barrel. Practice with the goal of learning to close the off eye while maintaining focus on the target.

Some people have a difficult time closing one eye when they shoot. This could be a problem if the off eye is affecting their ability to line up the barrels. One remedy is to put some frosted tape on your shooting glasses to block out the off eye once the gun is fully mounted. Shooting glasses can be

You can pick up the target with both eyes open . . .

. . . then, as you mount the gun, wink the off eye. This can be an effective option for a cross-dominant shooter.

custom made with a frosted spot to block out the off eye. The tape allows the shooter to acquire the target with both eyes at the start of the swing and mount. Once the mount is completed and the cheek is on the stock, the tape covers the off eye. So, in essence, you are using binocular vision to acquire the target, but the off eye is blocked out just before the mount is completed.

Here, an instructor is placing a piece of tape to block out the off eye.

The tape can also help new shooters develop a correct gun mount by allowing only the master eye to peer down the barrels.

Tape may not be the correct solution for a shooter who is extremely cross-eye dominant. In this case, the dominant eye will try to peer around the tape. This causes the head to twist and drop as the gun is mounted. In this case, it's best to see a professional shooting instructor for a personal solution. He may recommend switching shooting shoulders. This way, the master eye matches up with the correct shoulder. This may require a great deal of practice, but for someone who is extremely cross dominant, it may be the best long-term solution.

Eye dominance can greatly affect a shooter's performance in both positive and negative ways. Be sure that you have a solid understanding of how your eye dominance affects your overall shooting style and performance. Often a simple fix, such as winking an eye, can make all the difference.

The shooter can keep both eyes open to track the target.

As the gun is mounted, the tape blocks the off eye from taking over. The placement of the tape can be important.

13

What is the best shooting tip ever? Focus!

I'VE TAUGHT THOUSANDS THE ART AND CRAFT OF WING-shooting. I have coached countless beginners, seasoned veterans, and even Olympic competitors. What is the one tip that helps every shooter? The answer is *focus*. I'm talking about intense visual concentration on the target as it flies through the air. Visual concentration is not to be confused with visual acuity! Seeing well and focusing well are two different issues. I've seen shooters with Coke-bottle glasses who could shoot their competitors' lights out. The ability to visually concentrate is more a product of what goes on between the ears. Focus is the result of mental concentration. It's the ability to know how and where to look at a moving target.

It sounds almost overly simple, but the one tip that helps every shooter every time is improved focus. It works like this: You can't hope to hit a target that you clearly don't see. The key here is the word *clearly*. If the eyes are not focused squarely on the target, the hands and arms will not know where to point the shotgun. The pointing action of the hands is made easier when the eyes are locked in on the target.

At the Orvis School, I'll be working with a student who is having trouble with the most basic targets. I'll ask him what he saw when pulling the trigger. The answer on a miss is almost always: "I don't know."

At this point, I'll ask him to watch a few targets fly without shooting at them. Then, I'll ask him to look at something very specific on the clay. On a going-away target, I may ask him to look for the rings on the clay as it spins through the air. On a soft left to right crosser, I may have him look at the right edge of the clay. Once focused on the target, he simply locks in on that detail while mounting and shooting. Often on the very next shot, the clay is hit so completely that it turns to dust.

As a coach, I know when a shooter is having trouble focusing on the target. I watch how the barrels track the target through the air. If they wobble aimlessly around during the swing and mount, it's a sure sign that

Learning to focus the eye on the target and not the barrels is the key to shooting success.

the shooter's eyes are not locked on the clay. If the shooter's eyes are focused squarely on the target, the barrel swings in perfect harmony with it. Many times a shooter will say, "I knew I was going to hit that one." That's because the hands and body were completely in sync with the eyes. When the shooter has intense visual concentration on the clay, it is so much easier for the barrels to point out the target.

Missed shots occur when a bird hunter sees the trees and the sky. The bird is a bit of a blur as it flashes through the canopy. Missed clays often seem to be flying much faster than they really are. The real magic of looking for some detail on the clay is that it brings the target into sharper focus. The clay seems to be flying more slowly. It's as if you are in some kind of Zen zone: The eyes are so locked in on the target that you don't even notice the barrels as the gun comes up to the cheek and shoulder. All the shooter sees is the target exploding as the trigger is pulled. The duck hunter who downs a bird often only recalls seeing it fall out of the sky as the gun goes off. That is focus. It's almost as if the bird were highlighted in the air and the barrels were unnoticed in the background. The best shooters trust that the gun will shoot where the eyes are focused. That is a huge point for the shotgun shooter to understand. Focus is a skill that all shooters must work on.

The next time you are struggling with your shooting, sharpen your focus on the target. Look for some detail on the bird and avoid aiming with the barrel. If the target is in focus, you will have a much better chance of hitting it. Through practice and concentration, the art of focus can be mastered.

14

The sight picture—learn to tell time for better clay shooting

HAVE YOU EVER SHOT AT A CLAY TARGET AND JUST KNEW you were going to hit it? Why is that? Most likely, you had the correct sight picture. Think of the sight picture as a camera lens. How and what you focus on is your sight picture. On a miss, there is often a wide-angle focus. If you see the trees, sky, clouds, gun barrel, and target, that is a wide-ranging view. The sight picture is everywhere, but the focus is on nothing. The sight picture in this scenario lacks definition. A better sight picture is narrow, focused tightly on the target. Imagine the clay target in focus and everything else as just a backdrop. In other words, the target should be in high definition with the background out of focus.

The optimal sight picture gets even narrower. The focus is not just on the clay, but a specific part of it. Imagine looking at the leading edge of the target as it whizzes through the air. You're not just looking at the clay, you're focusing on a particular section of the target. At the Orvis Shooting Schools, we will often try to have students narrow their focus by imagining a clock face on the clay. Imagine twelve o'clock would be on top center and then six o'clock on the bottom center. Imagine nine o'clock as the left wing and three o'clock as the right wing. Often by narrowing your focus to a specific section of the clay, you can greatly improve your accuracy. Also, this can help a shooter understand the flight path and angle that the target is on. Say you are shooting a clay target that is flying away and quartering slightly, right to left. On this presentation, the leading edge would be nine o'clock. Frequently, just by having a student narrow their sight picture, they end up busting the target out of the sky. Also, depending on the fit of the gun, a shooter may be patterning a little low and more likely shooting a bit high. Again, let's look at the going away and slight right-to-left crosser. In a case in which the shooter is missing high, I have him focus on seven or eight o'clock. This allows the shooter to still be on the leading edge yet low enough to break the target.

The clock face analogy works on most presentations. The incoming target would put the focus on twelve o'clock or slightly ahead of twelve, depending on the speed and distance of the target. A quartering left-to-right shot that's slightly rising would require a two o'clock focus point.

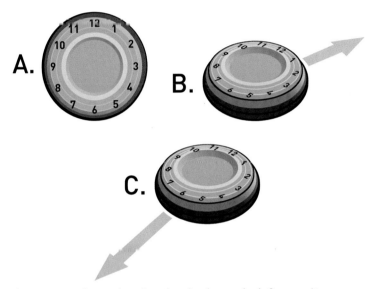

A: To sharpen your focus, imagine the clay has a clock face on it.
B: On a left-to-right crossing, focus your eye on the one or two o'clock spot on the clay. This should be the leading edge.
C: On a dropping bird, the eye might lock in on the six o'clock spot.

Many times, a shooter in the school will miss a basic quartering presentation. I'll ask them what he was focusing on when he was pulling the trigger. Often, the shooter tilts his head and says, "I'm not really sure." Then, I'll explain the clock face illustration and ask him to look at a specific number on the clay. On the very next shot, the clay will often explode into a puff of orange dust. The target is completely obliterated, and the student's eyes light up as if to say, "Aha! I have the right sight picture now!"

Learning to narrow the sight picture can help sharpen a shooter's focus and make busting clays seem routine.

Heightened concentration and focus is one of the most important skills a shooter can develop.

15

Picture your lead instinctively instead of measuring it

ON THE SHOOTING RANGE, YOU HEAR THESE WORDS uttered all the time: "Man, I was four feet in front of the target." Or, it could be, "I pulled three feet ahead of that bird!" Clay shooters are forever trying to figure out how far to lead a target. This is rarely helpful and only effective in games when you shoot the same presentation repeatedly. Measuring the lead with the gun muzzle is a difficult proposition. This will often make shooters focus on the barrels as they swing out ahead of the target. Once the focus is on the barrels, the swing and follow-through are compromised because the eyes can't focus on two objects at different distances. Once the eyes focus on the barrel, the swing and follow-through often stop. It's difficult to keep swinging with the target once the bird goes out of focus. This is due to the fact that the follow-through is stalled as you attempt to aim with the barrel.

Also, we all tend to perceive lead differently. Six inches of lead for one person may seem like two feet for someone else. So, when someone says to another shooter, "Shoot four feet ahead of the target," it most likely will not help.

How do you develop the correct lead or forward allowance when shooting? I always encourage shooters to picture the lead with the eyes rather than trying to measure it with the end of the gun. The shooter is aware that the barrels are ahead of the bird, but his focus is still on the target. The target is clear and the shooter is aware of the barrels, but he is not distracted by or focused on them. This is what is meant by developing an instinctive lead. It can be difficult for some shooters to adapt to this method of shooting, but with practice, any shooter can easily learn to picture the lead without aiming with the barrels.

The easiest way to develop instinctive lead is to swing through the target. Come from behind, and then overtake the flying bird. This way, the speed

Picture the lead instinctively: You should be aware of the muzzle ahead, but the focus should still be on the bird.

of the target compels you to swing out ahead of it. As long as you keep your focus on the path of the bird and not on the barrels, you should be able to picture the correct lead. If the target is flying hard and fast, your swing will have to be aggressive and fast to overtake the bird. The speed of the bird will help you swing ahead of the target effectively.

This is a better way to develop the correct forward allowance. Measuring all the different leads needed for every target, angle, and speed would be impossible. This is especially true for the wingshooter. Birds can flush and fly in a myriad of angles, with different speeds and distances. It often seems that no two birds fly alike. The wingshooter is best advised to develop the correct forward allowance naturally.

When coaching shooters, I almost always know when they are aiming with the barrels. How? I'm not clairvoyant, but the swing and follow-through tell it all. Often, on the longer crossing shots, you will need to lead the target a bit more. Frequently, after a few misses, a student will try to figure out where he is missing by aiming with the barrels. This is a natural reaction. The mind wants to know: Where am I missing? This is when there is a temptation to measure or calculate the lead precisely. Once the barrels stop swinging, I know that the student's eyes are choosing to focus on the end of the gun and not on the target. This is when I ask the shooter to trust his natural reflexes. I have him swing through the bird and picture the lead without focusing on the muzzle. I want the shooter to be aware that he is ahead of the target without calculating the lead with the gun barrel. It is amazing how accurately one can shoot when he learns to trust his natural reflexes. The swing and follow-through become almost effortless. The gun swings ahead of the bird, and the shot is taken at the perfect moment. Because the eyes are not distracted by the gun, the follow-through is smooth and clean.

Measuring lead: the focus is clearly on the barrels. Often, to hit the target, you'll have to perceive much more lead this way.

PART

IV

Basic Shotgun Know-How

16

Choose the right gauge

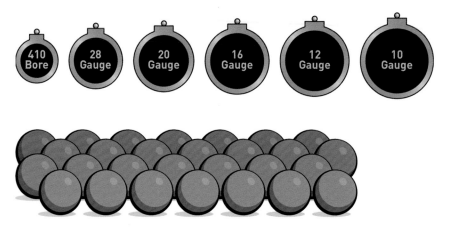

It takes twenty-eight lead balls of the same diameter as the twenty-eight-gauge barrel to equal one pound.

CHOOSING THE RIGHT GAUGE CAN BE A CONFUSING proposition. The most basic question to be asked is, what type of shooting do you intend to do the most? From there, you should select a gauge that is best suited for that task. Let's begin by exploring various shotgun gauges and the ideal purpose of each.

Shotguns are classified by gauge (except the .410, which is actually a caliber) unlike handguns and rifles, which are classified by caliber. The way shotgun gauges are determined dates back hundreds of years. It is an out-of-date and antiquated way to measure the gauge of a gun, but it's still the industry standard.

The term gauge refers to the bore diameter of the shotgun. Generally speaking, there are six common shotgun gauges. These are the ten-gauge, twelve-gauge, twenty-gauge, sixteen-gauge, twenty-eight-gauge, and the .410. The .410 is the only shotgun classified by caliber rather than by gauge.

The ten-gauge is the largest of modern gauges, and the .410 is the smallest. The most common shotgun gauges used for wingshooting today are the twelve-gauge, the twenty-gauge, and the twenty-eight-gauge. Each gauge is determined by the number of equal-sized lead balls the diameter of the bore it would take to weigh a pound. In twelve-gauge, it takes twelve lead balls of the same diameter to equal one pound.

What does all this mean? The gauge (and smaller the number designation), the more pellets, or shot, that can be fit into each cartridge or shell. If you are goose hunting, you might want more and larger pellets to help take down these big birds effectively. If you're hunting rabbits or quail, you will want more and smaller pellets to create a wider, more effective shot pattern. It's about finding the right balance, so that you can effectively hit the target without resorting to overkill.

Taking game cleanly is an ethical matter. You want to kill the animal or bird cleanly, not destroy it. For this reason, it's important to choose a shotgun gauge that can take game cleanly without undue damage or loss.

Also, there's the matter of recoil to consider when selecting a shotgun. Generally, larger gauges tend to produce the most recoil. Most sporting clay enthusiasts tend to choose the twelve-gauge because it gives them a higher concentration of pellets and a denser pattern, but it can be tiring to shoot a twelve-gauge for multiple ten-round sessions. A shooter of slight build and lighter weight may find it difficult to absorb the recoil of the twelve-gauge during a prolonged shooting session. A smaller shotgun such as a twenty- or twenty-eight-gauge produces an effective pattern and results in much less recoil. I often feel beat up after shooting fifty or 100 rounds with a twelve-gauge. I would much rather shoot a smaller gauge shotgun and not have to deal with the after effects of excessive recoil at the end of the day.

17

Don't confuse shotgun gauge with pattern size

IT'S IMPORTANT TO NOTE THAT A SHOTGUN'S GAUGE HAS nothing to do with pattern size. New shooters often think that a twelve-gauge produces a larger pattern or spread of pellets than a twenty-eight-gauge. This is not the case. The constriction at the end of the barrel is what determines how wide the pattern of pellets will be. Most modern shotguns have interchangeable chokes that screw in at the end of the barrel. It is the choke that determines how your shotguns will pattern, usually measured by firing at a thirty-inch circle at a distance of thirty yards.

Generally speaking, if you have twelve- and twenty-eight-gauge shotguns with the same choke constriction and shot size, they will produce the same *size* pattern at thirty yards. The twelve-gauge would have a *denser* pattern, or more pellets inside the circle. This is due to the fact that a twelve-gauge shell contains more shot because of its larger capacity.

Oddly enough, a .410 shooting No. 9 shot will open up its pattern of pellets much faster than a twelve-gauge shooting No. 3 shot. This is true even if both barrels have the same choke constriction.

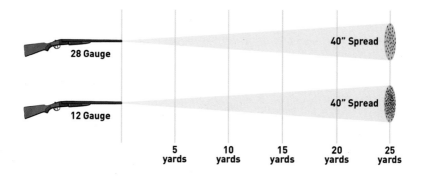

A twenty-eight-gauge and a twelve-gauge shooting the same choke will have the same pattern size at twenty-five to thirty yards. The twelve-gauge will have greater pellet density due to its larger shell, but the pattern size will be similar.

18

How to read a box
of shells

WHEN YOU LOOK AT A BOX OF SHELLS, THERE ARE SEVERAL numbers listed on it. What do they all mean?

The first item to look for is the gauge designation—twelve, twenty-eight, twenty, and so on. The next item is the length of the shell. Most shells made for target shooting are 2¾ inches long. Most modern shotguns have three-inch chambers. Some even have 3½-inch chambers. Be aware that many older guns may have two- or 2½-inch chambers. This information is usually found stamped on the side of the gun's barrel. It's OK to shoot shorter shells in longer chambers, but never try to shoot longer shells in shotguns with shorter chambers. If you don't know a shotgun's chamber length, take it to a reputable gunsmith and have it checked out.

Next, there is dram equivalent or Dr. Eq., listed next to the shot charge, which is measured in ounces. Dram equivalent is an older term that refers to how much black powder it would take to replace the smokeless powder charge. Dram equivalent is out-of-date terminology because black powder is no longer used in modern ammunition.

Many manufacturers are switching to feet per second or fps. This refers to how fast the pellets are traveling when they leave the muzzle. It is also referred to as muzzle velocity. This is commonly somewhere between 1,100 fps to 1,400 fps in most modern shotgun shells.

The charge of shot is listed in ounces and is typically ¾ ounce up to sometimes 1¼ ounce in target loads. As we'll discuss later, more is not always better. For example, heavier loads produce heavier recoil. For new shooters, this can be very uncomfortable during a long session at the range.

The last number of importance on a box of shells is shot size. The higher the number, the smaller the pellet size. The smaller gauges typically carry the smaller shot sizes. Most common in a twenty-eight-gauge is No. 8 and No. 9 shot. A twelve-gauge shotgun can handle anything from

7½ to BBB. The largest-size shotgun pellets are listed as B, BB, and BBB. The accompanying chart (page 57) should help clear up any confusion.

Study all the information listed on a box of shells before you make your purchase. I've had friends show up to hunt with shells of the wrong gauge. It's tough to shoot a twenty-eight-gauge if you only have twenty-gauge shells!

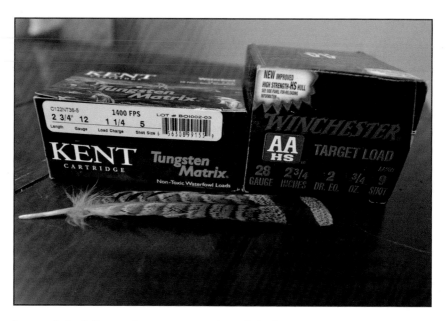

Learn what all the numbers mean on a box of shells.

19

Understand the shot string

INTERESTINGLY, THE SHOT OF A SHOTGUN DOESN'T FLY out flat like a pancake, nor do all pellets arrive at the target at the same time. Shotgun pellets not only expand in circumference but in length as well. The shotgun pattern is more like a cylinder, the shape of a trash can, flying through the air. This elongated cylinder is commonly referred to as the shot string.

The circumference of patterns remains consistent between gauges, but the length of the shot string can vary greatly. There are several factors that determine how long the shot string will become in flight. The size of the pellets and the amount of force (or powder load used) to propel them can greatly affect the length of the shot string. These two factors, along with gauge or bore size, determine how the shot string develops. Generally, the smaller the shot size and bore diameters in combination with heavier loads, the longer the shot string. Also, softer and smaller pellets tend to create an exceedingly long shot string. In addition, softer pellets tend to deform as they travel down the barrel. Deformed pellets are ineffective flyers and tend to spiral out of the shot pattern. To minimize the effects of shot deformity, purchase good-quality ammo. Harder pellets tend to be more expensive because they are made with premium alloy and usually include a one-piece shot cup with "wings" that protect the shot load as it travels down the barrel and through the choke constriction. In competition, quality loads can be well worth the price because they are more effective at holding the pattern together and, as a result, deliver more pellets to the target.

An excessively long shot string can be ineffective at taking game because a higher percentage of pellets don't get to the target on time. A shorter, more compact shot string delivers more pellets effectively to the target, producing fewer wounded birds and more clean kills.

The shot string is how the pellets spread apart over distances.

20

Shot size can greatly affect success in the field

ONE SEASON, SOME WATERFOWLING FRIENDS AND I WERE set up in a bay on Lake Ontario. A lone bufflehead came in low and fast. Captain Bill Saiff barked out, "Take 'em, Tommy!" I jumped up and took my shot. The bird folded up and bounced twice atop the water like a skipping rock. After the bird landed on the water, it righted itself and took off flying. I was stunned! I shook my head in disbelief. I thought that my shot had cleanly killed the bird.

"What kind of shells are you shooting?" Bill asked me. I looked in my bag for a shell. I was using No. 5.

"These ducks are pretty tough," Saiff said. "No. 3 shells would be a better choice."

That day was a real eye-opener for me. It was my first time shooting sea ducks or "white ducks," as Saiff called them. After that day on Lake Ontario, I paid more attention to shot size when it came to which game I was hunting.

Shot size refers to the size of the pellets contained—the higher the number, the smaller the shot size. For example, BB shot is a larger projectile than a No. 8 pellet. The larger shot sizes are used to take larger game. For example, 00 Buckshot is ideal for large game such as deer, whereas No. 9 shot is perfect for fragile birds such as woodcock or quail. A goose hunter would generally use No. 1 shot or BBs. The woodcock or quail hunter would tend to favor the smaller pellets sizes, such as a 7½ or 8. A duck hunter may use anything from No. 6 or No. 4 all the way up to No. 2, depending on the situation. A waterfowl hunter in flooded timber may have shots at ducks coming in much closer than a hunter shooting at eiders on more open water.

Keep in mind that pellets of various sizes tend to perform differently even when shot out of the same choke or bore diameter. The larger shot sizes tend to stay together longer, and the smaller pellets tend to open up a little more quickly. I have patterned different shot sizes through the same barrel constriction, and the results were dramatic. This can work to the shooter's advantage. On smaller birds like quail, you generally want the pattern to open to its maximum efficiency around thirty-five to forty-five yards. Smaller pellets open quickly and provide more density in your pattern at close range. The last thing you want on smaller game is a pattern with holes in it. When duck hunting, you may be shooting at the edge of your decoy spread. Some days, forty yards is the closest shot. No. 3 or No. 4 shot can hold its pattern at a much longer range than No. 7½ or No. 8 shot.

Try patterning different loads and shot sizes through your shotgun. You may be surprised at the difference you see at twenty, thirty, and forty yards.

Another point to consider is that larger shot sizes tend to transfer more energy and inflict more damage upon impact. Imagine two lead balls traveling at 800 feet per second. One is the size of a pea, and the other is the size of a bowling ball. Which would do more damage if it hit a car door? Clearly, the larger object would create much more damage. This is true of shot size as well. Consider what happens when a swarm of No. 2 pellets hits a duck versus when a light load of No. 9 shot hits it. When clay target shooting, shot size is not nearly as important because it takes only one pellet to break the brittle clay.

Adjust your shot size to maximize the effectiveness of your pattern.

The bird hunter should pay much more attention to the size of the pellets he selects. Generally, choose the smallest shot size that will do the job effectively. Too small a shot size will mean more cripples, whereas larger shot sizes will inflict excessive damage.

21

Get the lowdown on the load charge

THERE ARE MANY FACTORS AND CONFIGURATIONS TO consider when buying shot shells. Pellet size, pellet hardness, bore diameter, and load charge are designed to create the ideal shotgun pattern. Load often refers to the powder charge, or amount of gunpowder used in the shell. When the powder charge is ignited by the primer, the resulting explosion propels the shot through the barrel.

The most common shot charges are ⅞ oz., 1 oz., 1⅛ oz., and 1¼ oz. The smaller gauge shells have less of a load charge in them, which is why they have less recoil.

Often, the bird hunter thinks the heavier the load, the better. A heavier load charge does produce more shot speed at the muzzle—pellets can fly upwards to 1,400 fps. This is also called muzzle velocity. It is interesting to note what happens to all this speed down range. Often, the pellets in heavier loads can lose up to 60 percent of their velocity at forty yards. Shot pellets that started out at 1,400 fps would be flying around 800 fps at forty yards.

Let's look at a lighter load that starts out at 1,200 fps, and let's say they lose 60 percent velocity at forty yards. So, $1,200 \times 60\% = 720$ fps. The difference between the two loads at forty yards is only eighty feet per second! I'm generalizing here, but if you look at the information contained in any reloading manual, you'll see that the numbers are similar. Velocity is not that important at the muzzle. What matters more is down-range kinetic energy, which is best achieved by using a larger pellet size. Remember, larger pellets have more mass, and more mass tends to mean more energy. A pattern of No. 1 shot traveling at 700 fps could do more damage than twice the number of No. 8 traveling at the same speed.

Heavier loads also deform some pellets. The initial explosion in the chamber will deform the pellets in the back of the pack as well as those closest to the barrel walls. These deformed pellets fly poorly and tend to spin out of the pattern. This effect is less common today thanks to better designs in shot cups and harder shot compounds, but some deformation is inevitable in standard target and hunting loads.

Heavier loads (often called magnum loads) tend to recoil a lot more. This makes shooting more difficult, especially when you are trying to reacquire a target with your second shot. A gun that kicks wildly will often be a distraction if you are not used to it. Heavy loads are tough to shoot all day, especially in 100-round sporting clays events. Again, at forty yards, there is not that big of a difference between standard target loads and magnum loads, so why beat yourself up?

In fact, many target loads are great for taking game. A twenty-eight-gauge target load of No. 9 shot with a maximum dram equivalent of powder is just fine for shooting quail at ranges under twenty-five yards. A twelve-gauge target load with No. 6 shot can be very effective when shooting at pheasants.

Understanding shot and powder charges and performance can help you select the proper shells for the job and may even improve your success at the range or in the field.

22

Shooting glasses are a must

EVERYONE SHOULD WEAR SHOOTING GLASSES WHEN operating any firearm. It's a question of safety. Every time you pull the trigger on a live round, an explosion occurs in the chamber of the shotgun. The blast is just inches from the shooter's eyes. As safe as modern shotgun designs are, there is always the potential for accidents. Wear shooting glasses every time you plan to shoot.

In nearly twenty years of coaching at the Orvis Wingshooting Schools, we have never had an incident, but I do hear stories. The most common story is how a shooter inadvertently loaded his chapstick into the chamber. Somehow, the tube ends up in his hunting vest pocket and gets mixed in with the shells. In the heat of the moment, the shooter quickly reloads because more birds are holding tight nearby. The smaller chapstick tube slides down the barrel and the gun fails to fire. Another shell is hastily loaded into the chamber. This results in a blockage of the barrel that causes a nasty explosion. I've seen the aftermath of such blockages many times. The same thing occurs when a shooter mistakenly loads a twenty-gauge shell into a twelve-gauge shotgun.

I'll visit the gunsmith shop, and the guys will show me a set of barrels that look like the twisted metal of a car wreck. Typically the damage occurs just past the chamber. Anyone who has witnessed this or has seen a set of barrels blown apart will understand why it is important to *always* wear safety glasses.

Another practical reason to wear shooting glasses is that they can help the shooter see the target more clearly. Often, light conditions make it difficult to pick up the target. The right tint in your shooting glasses makes it much easier to see a bird darting through the foliage. Picking up a clay target can also be tough at times. Tinted shooting glasses can help make the clay target more visible against the backdrop of trees or a somber sky.

I always wear shooting glasses when I coach. They help me pick up even the subtlest details when I'm peeking over a shooter's shoulder, and they really help me pick up the placement of the shot string on a miss.

Some shooting glasses are sold with a variety of interchangeable colored lenses. This way, you can simply switch them out as conditions dictate. I like my hunting lens photochromic. This way, the lens adjusts automatically to the light conditions. If the sun is bright, the lens tint becomes darker, whereas in low light, the lenses become perfectly clear.

I wear shooting glasses while duck hunting so that I can see clearly as I'm steering the outboard or tossing decoys. As morning progresses, the lenses adjust again as the sun comes up bright and clear. This way I don't have to switch lenses as light conditions change.

It may seem silly to point out, but shooting glasses are made for shooting. Most fashion eye glasses are not! Be aware that small-framed glasses may not be suitable for shooting. As you mount the gun, the eyes tend to roll up to the top eyelid. Smaller framed eyeglasses have a lower profile, which can be a problem. I have seen shooters look right over the top of their glasses as they mount the shotgun. Shooting glasses are designed with a higher, wider profile, so that a shooter can still see through them even as the head tilts onto the stock. If you are serious about shotgunning, arrange to be fitted for a pair of quality shooting glasses.

Shooting glasses should be worn in the field and on the clay range.

23

How to reduce recoil

NOTHING CAN RUIN AN AFTERNOON OF SHOOTING MORE than a gun that kicks like a mule with steel-toed hooves. A gun that has excessive recoil can be unpleasant to shoot, especially when you are shooting a round of 100 sporting clays.

Recoil is a byproduct of the explosion that occurs when the shotgun is fired. How much a gun kicks is determined by the weight of the gun and the load contained within the shell.

At the Orvis Shooting Schools, we tend to do a lot of shooting, and all that shooting can add up to a sore shoulder if you are not careful. When a new female shooter arrives, one who is petite and weighs around 130 pounds soaking wet, I'm not going to hand her a twelve-gauge shotgun to use for the next two days. We put new shooters in smaller gauges because they are simply more comfortable to shoot.

The sub-gauge shotguns are normally lighter in weight, so we use reduced loads. A twenty-eight-gauge gun with ¾-ounce load is a very pleasant gun to handle and shoot. A twenty-eight-gauge shotgun is about two to 2½ pounds lighter than a twelve-gauge gun. This makes it easier to carry in the woods and has much less recoil when fired.

It's a good idea to start a new shooter with a lighter-gauge gun, but there will be some felt recoil still. In some cases, a lighter gun can make the problem worse. The gun must fit the shooter somewhat to reduce felt recoil. Often, kids or female shooters are given a lighter gauge to try out, but if the gun doesn't fit them correctly, it may have quite a bit of kick to it. A lighter gun that is too short may actually kick more than a standard twelve-gauge that fits properly. A fitted gun allows the shooter to absorb recoil more effectively and is more comfortable to shoot over long periods.

Have you ever heard the saying, "It's the pilot not the plane"? How you handle a gun can affect how much recoil you feel. Think of it as pilot error, so to speak. A proper gun mount puts the body in the correct position to absorb the recoil. The butt of the gun is placed in the shoulder pocket. The shooter's weight is slightly forward, and the stock is pressed into the cheek.

When the gun is fired, everything is snug and secure. The body is able to absorb the blast from the gun.

The problem occurs when a shooter mounts the gun incorrectly. This occurs when he becomes tired after a long session of shooting. The head and body begin to pull away from the gun in anticipation of the recoil. Unfortunately, this only makes the recoil feel more intense. As the shooter pulls away, it gives the gun more room to move. That little bit of space, provided because the shooter pulls away, allows the gun to kick into the shoulder and cheek with more force.

The closer you are to the gun when it fires, the easier it is for the body to absorb the recoil. Imagine lying on your back and having a five-pound brick dropped on your shoulder. If it's dropped from a millimeter away, you would hardly feel it. However, if it falls from three feet, away you would certainly feel it a lot more. Keep the gun in your shoulder and your cheek on the stock, and you'll feel less recoil.

Finally, consider using an autoloader to help reduce felt recoil. Autos, particularly gas-operated autoloaders, tend to produce less recoil. This is because some of the recoil is absorbed in the operation of the gun. Some energy is used to eject the spent shell and load the next one. Such shotguns can be helpful to shooters who are sensitive to recoil.

I have a friend who had a shoulder injury. He gave up shooting because his shoulder could not handle the recoil. He ended up trying a friend's autoloader and loved it, so he bought one for himself. He had the stock custom fitted and attached a recoil pad (which also helps, but only marginally). The end result was a soft-shooting gun that he could shoot accurately.

Shooting a shotgun doesn't have to be an uncomfortable sporting event. Find ways to reduce felt recoil, and you will enjoy a more pleasant shooting experience.

Please refer to the photos on the next page for a graphic illustration of recoil and its effect.

If you look closely at these photos, you can see how much the gun is recoiling back into the shoulder (photo B), and that the head is pushed off the stock (photo C).

24

Wear some hearing protection

HEARING PROTECTION IS A MUST IF YOU ARE SHOOTING firearms of any kind. I've been a professional shooting instructor for almost twenty years and still have most of my hearing.

When I learned to handle a shotgun, my tutors handed out hearing protection immediately, but this was not always the case. One of my shooting mentors, Dave Sholem, told me a story about his shooting club back in the 1950s. He said they would shoot skeet and trap all day, and no one wore hearing protection. When I met Sholem in the early 1990s, he had poor hearing and had to read lips to understand his students.

Times have changed, and hearing protection is standard issue, with good reason. Hearing loss is really nerve damage, which means it's irreversible. Most hearing aids merely amplify sound and will not help a person with severe nerve damage. Even the most modern and expensive hearing aids that can filter background noise and boost speech frequencies do little to help permanent hearing loss.

The odds are that if you are exposed to frequent loud, concussive blasts, you will eventually have some type of hearing loss. I've been told by audiologists that high-decibel sound waves can travel through nasal passages and even through your mouth if it is open. These sound waves can affect the inner ear and lead to nerve damage.

The most basic type of hearing protection is the little moldable foam pieces that you stick in your ear. You simply roll them up to reduce their size and they expand once they are in your ear. These are effective at blocking the noise once they expand in the ear, but they can be harmful to your ear canal if used frequently, as they can push the wax in your ear farther back into the ear canal, causing irritation. Even though they are effective at blocking noise, some shooters find the foam insert–type ear plugs to be inconvenient.

Many shooters opt for ear muff–style hearing protection. Most of these can be effective at blocking out harmful sounds, and they tend not to irritate the ears. They come in a variety of styles, but most shooters prefer the low-profile type that won't interfere with the gun mount.

Sometimes, even the most comfortable ear muff-style hearing protection can be cumbersome. Some shooters, depending on how they mount the gun, can feel the ear muff as they press the gun into the shoulder and cheek. The stock bumps into the ear muffs as the mount is completed. Sometimes, they can even interfere with the gun mount. Although these events are rare, some shooters find ear muff style hearing protection to be annoying.

The most modern type of hearing protection fits comfortably into the ear canal and is nearly invisible. Some manufacturers even mold the hearing protection to conform to the shape of the individual's ear. Some units allow the shooters to hear everything that's going on around them but cut off the sound once it reaches a certain decibel level. So, you could be sitting in a duck blind listening to your buddy tell boring stories about how great his dog is, and then once the shooting starts, your ear protection cuts off the sound of gunfire.

I've used the ear muff–style protection with this type of technology, and it worked very well. However, recently, I had a custom pair made for my ears. It fits like a glove and is comfortable to use. I still can hear conversations, but loud shotgun blasts are blocked.

Hearing protection is a must if you are shooting a shotgun.

25

Understand the shell game

THE MODERN SHOTGUN SHELL HAS DRAMATICALLY improved over the years. Today's shells are vastly superior, particularly to the paper shells made in the 1940s and 1950s. In the early 1960s, Remington Arms led the way by introducing a shell made of brass, steel, and plastic. Their developments in materials led to a revolution of sorts in the manufacture of shotgun shells. Earlier shells had a paper case and paper wads. The biggest drawback to this type of shell was that it wasn't waterproof and was often prone to swelling. Duck hunters had many problems with extraction, ejection, and magazine functioning using those early paper shells.

The single most important factor in shotshell design, at least in my opinion, was the development of the plastic wad or cup. The wad essentially cushions and surrounds the shot pellets as they travel down the bore. This led to more accurate shooting due to improved pattern density. Before the plastic wad was developed, shotgun pellets would deform more easily as they scraped against the metal of the barrel. This was because the lead pellets of the era were softer

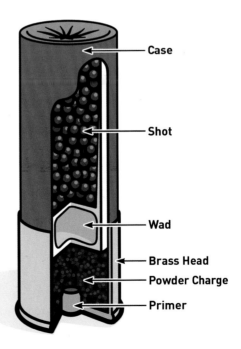

Parts a of shotgun shell.

than the steel barrel. Deformed pellets would tend to spin out of the shot string before reaching the target, leading to reduced pattern density.

The plastic wad also did a much better job of starting the pellets down the bore. The illustration above outlines the various parts of the shell. It is important to understand how each component works to effectively move the pellets out of the barrel.

P A R T

V

Gun Fit

26

To shoot well, be fitted for a shotgun

A fitted gun becomes an extension of the shooter's eyes and hands.

WHAT IS GUN FITTING AND WHY SHOULD A SHOOTER care about shotgun fit? Both are valid questions. Gun fitting creates a set of stock dimensions for the individual shooter and a gun that suits the build and physique of an individual. It creates a gun that becomes an extension of the shooter's eyes and hands. A properly fitted shotgun shoots where your eyes are focused. The gun then naturally becomes easier to point and shoot.

This is crucial for the shotgun shooter because wild birds and clay targets often fly fast and unpredictably. The seasoned shotgunner does not aim with the muzzle. There is simply no time to line up the barrels on a fast-flying target whizzing through the trees. When the shooter does try to aim, the target is often lost. The split second that the eye takes to focus on the bead allows the target to escape. In all my years as a coach, I have never seen an effective shooter who aims with the end of the barrel. Shooters who try to aim always lose that split-second connection with the flight path of the target.

A formal gun fitting is similar to having a custom suit made. During the process, the shotgun stock is specifically tailored to your unique build. Certainly, you could just wear a forty-four regular that seems to fit nicely. However, what if you are a forty-three short and your gun is a forty-six tall? Most manufacturers create stocks that fit the ubiquitous "average guy." However, most off-the-rack stocks will not fit the majority of shooters. A fitted gun also typically has less felt recoil and is easier to mount.

A properly fitted shotgun allows the shooter to make an almost effortless connection with the bird. Swing mount and shot placement become harmoniously synchronized with the point of focus. Anyone who shoots a shotgun will benefit from a professional gun fitting.

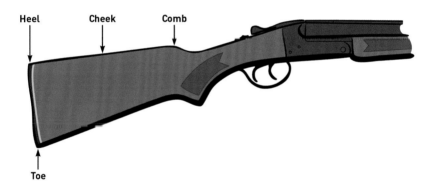

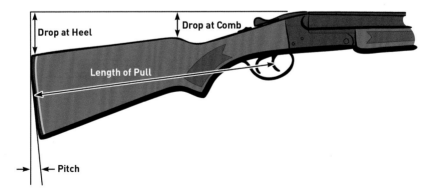

Elements of gunfit.

27

Pattern your shotgun!

SHOOTING A SHOTGUN IS AN EDUCATION. IN MOST OTHER sports, the participant can easily identify some of his own mistakes. In shot-gunning, however, it is difficult to determine how you may be missing the target. It is next to impossible to see one's own shot string as it sails over or under the clay target. An experienced shooter can sometimes guess how he is missing a target, but even then it is only a hunch. When you are just starting out, it can be difficult to diagnose your misses.

In golf, if a player is missing the fairway to the right, it's called a slice, which is caused by certain factors in the golfer's swing. Armed with this information, a golfer can correct his swing. The shotgun shooter often cannot self-correct without some knowledge of where that shot pattern is going.

It's a good idea to pattern your shotgun, especially if the stock has not been fitted to you. And even if your stock has been custom tailored to you, it's still a good idea to shoot your gun at a patterning board every so often. Patterning a shotgun gives the shooter direct feedback on his point of impact. This can give the shooter invaluable knowledge about where the shot pattern is going astray on its way to the target. Often, a right-handed shooter with an off-the-rack shotgun will tend to miss high and a little left. This is great on a rising target going to the left, but it can be a real handicap on targets going to the right. If you know how your gun patterns you can be better prepared for each shot.

A patterning board is a metal sheet painted white with a target in the center. This type of patterning board is often used during a gun fitting to determine the point of impact for the shooter. A shot at the board reveals where the pellets are landing in relation to the target and point of aim. Some whitewash paint is simply splashed over the pattern, and it can be shot at again.

Most shooting clubs have patterning boards available to members or guests. However, if you don't have access to a patterning board, you can create one out of hay bales and sheets of paper. Large paper pattern sheets with birds as targets can be easily found in sporting goods stores or on the Internet. Simply stack up a few hay bales to create a makeshift patterning board and place the paper patterning sheets on them. I like to have the patterning board slightly higher than eye level. Most shooting occurs on targets that are rising, so this makes it a little more natural to mount the gun.

There are a few simple rules to remember when patterning your shotgun. It's important to follow these rules if you want an accurate indication of where your gun is shooting. First, stand sixteen yards from the target. This should give you an adequate distance to accurately assess the shotgun pattern. At the Orvis schools, we do all of our fittings at this distance. If you are off a little, it's no big deal. As long as you are around sixteen yards, you should be able to get an effective reading. I like to use a tight choke such as modified or full. This gives you a dense pattern, and it can show you where the miss is in relation to the target.

Shoot at the patterning board as you would at a moving target. Avoid aiming the gun and use a proper gun mount while focusing on the target. Pull the trigger after you have a full gun mount, but before you are tempted to aim.

The gun mount plays a large part in how your gun patterns. If you have a consistent gun mount, you'll get a more consistent pattern.

I would not recommend that anyone alter his stock until he has developed a consistent and proper gun mount. Following these steps will give you the most accurate indication of where your gun is patterning.

28

Use a try gun for the perfect fit

THE TRY GUN IS THE TOOL OF THE PROFESSIONAL GUN fitter. It is an interesting feat of engineering. It has a normal action and barrels like other shotguns, but the stock is fully adjustable. This allows the fitter to adjust the stock to suit the build and shooting form of each individual shooter. The stock may be shortened or lengthened; the comb may be raised or lowered. The stock may even be bent to the left or right for adjustments called "cast." The end result is a stock that is perfectly tailored to the shooter.

The Try Gun may be adjusted in increments as small as $\frac{1}{16}$ to $\frac{1}{8}$ of an inch. This can be done very quickly with just a couple of twists of an Allen wrench. The shooter can quickly see the results of the fitter's adjustments on the patterning board. The point of impact may be dialed in so that the shooter's focal point and the barrels are in perfect alignment. The patterning board is a real eye-opener for students. They can see how the gun mount and stock adjustments affect the point of impact in their own shooting.

The key elements of gun fit are length of pull, pitch, drop, and cast. It's important to note that each element can have an effect on another. Pitch affects length of pull, and length can affect drop, so each dimension is dependent upon the other. As a gun fitter, I begin with pitch and length of pull. This establishes a baseline from which I can adjust drop and cast. This creates a stock of the proper length that the shooter can mount comfortably. At this point, the other dimensions can be dialed in.

Some shooters come to the Orvis School having already made adjustments to their shotguns. Most of the time, the length of pull is shortened or lengthened for the shooter. This may have only addressed one small piece of the gun fitting puzzle. Drop at heel and cast have a much greater effect on the point of impact. Also, merely making an adjustment to the length of pull can sometimes make matters worse.

It can be difficult to find a professional gun fitter who uses a Try Gun to conduct fittings, but it is worth the time it takes to track one down for a professional fitting. It is interesting to see all the elements of gun fit put into action with a Try Gun.

The Try Gun is the tool of the professional gun fitter.

29

Understanding length of pull

LENGTH OF PULL SIMPLY MEANS HOW LONG THE STOCK IS. It is the measurement from the middle of the trigger to the middle of the butt stock. If the shotgun has double triggers, the measurement is taken from the first trigger.

The correct length of pull helps a shooter to consistently mount the gun correctly to the shoulder and cheek. A gun that is too short often exhibits excessive recoil and creates a tendency for the shooter to drop his head during the gun mount. Head movement during the mount is a leading cause of misses for many shooters.

A stock that is too long is difficult to mount smoothly and often causes a gun to shoot too high. This happens because the gun cannot be fully mounted to the shoulder and cheek. When this happens, the eye is too high in relation to the end of the gun. The barrels come up to meet the eye, and as a result, the shot sails over the target.

The length of pull is too often overanalyzed. So many times a shooter will select a shotgun based on the length of pull without considering drop or cast. Length of pull is just one piece of the gun-fitting puzzle.

A shooter will take a gun out of the gun rack and try a few dry mounts. He envisions birds flushing and then shoulders the gun to see how it comes up. This is fun to do, I admit. I do this too if I see a neat little gun that catches my eye. The problem is that this doesn't tell you much about how the stock fits.

Length of pull is the most forgiving of all the elements involved in gun fit. A shooter could handle a gun that is up to ½ inch short and still shoot it well. The same holds true for a gun that is slightly too long. Most shooters can handle a shotgun that's ⅛ to ¼ inch too long. Any longer than that and mounting becomes difficult.

There is much less tolerance for errors in drop and cast. It's nearly impossible to accurately shoot a gun when the cast or drop is off by more than ⅛ inch.

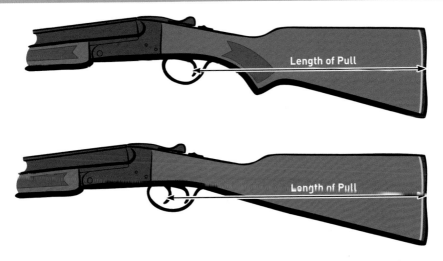

The length of pull is the measurement from the middle trigger to the middle of the butt stock. If the gun happens to have double triggers, then the measurement is taken from the first trigger.

This gun seems too long for the shooter. A gun that is too long can cause problems when mounting.

This gun appears to be too short for this shooter. The head appears to be too forward on the comb.

This gun is the proper length for the shooter. The correct length of pull leads to a more accurate shot and a more consistent gun mount.

It's comforting to know that there is some wiggle room concerning the length of the stock, but developing a consistent gun mount requires a proper length of pull. The proper length of pull allows the shooter to consistently mount the gun with correct form. A properly fitted stock effortlessly comes to the shoulder and cheek. The body and head do not need to make adjustments for the stock length. The shotgun slides into position and the eyes remain steady on the target. Therefore, the correct length of pull improves a shooter's focus in many ways. The head can remain steady, keeping the eyes locked in on the bird.

There are many factors that determine the proper length of pull. It can depend on the length of your arms, the thickness of your chest, and the length of your neck. There are also other factors besides your physical features that play a part in determining your length of pull. Your gun mounting style can have a great impact on stock length: A shooter who extends the neck and mounts the gun firmly may need a longer stock than someone who holds the head high and gently mounts the gun.

Even where you place the lead hand on the forend can affect the length of pull. A bird hunter may hold his lead hand way out on the forend, which can make the gun feel longer, so a slightly shorter stock maybe more suitable. A clay shooter may prefer to place his lead hand farther back on the forend, which allows the gun to be drawn out more with the lead hand. In this case, a longer length of pull may be helpful.

The best way to develop a proper gun mount is to shoot a gun with the correct length stock. A proper gun mount can only be developed when your shotgun stock fits your mounting style and individual build. Bad habits in gun mount are developed when a shooter tries to shoot a shotgun with a poor fit. Begin with the appropriate length stock, and you will develop a consistent and proper gun mount.

30

Make sure you have the proper pitch on the butt of the stock

PITCH IS THE ANGLE ON THE BUTT OF THE STOCK IN relation to the barrels. Proper pitch allows the butt to lie comfortably on the shoulder as the gun is mounted. A butt stock with the wrong pitch can cause misses and be uncomfortable to shoot because the toe of the stock digs into the upper chest every time the gun goes off.

← Pitch

Having the proper pitch can make a significant difference in your shooting abilities.

Think of it in simple terms: If the butt of the stock is set at zero, then the angle between the barrel and the butt is ninety degrees. Imagine if the toe is cut back more than the heel on the butt. This creates what is called positive pitch. If the angle of the butt stock is eighty-nine degrees in relation to the barrels, that would be +1 degree. An eighty-seven–degree angle or cut in the butt stock would be +3 degrees. You can do the math from here. On average, most field stocks have anywhere from +3 to +5 degrees of pitch.

The flip side of the issue is negative pitch. This is when the angle between the butt of the gun and the barrel exceeds ninety degrees. For example, ninety-one degrees would be -1 degree of pitch. Negative pitch can cause the toe of the stock to dig into the shoulder upon completion of the gun mount.

I have seen trap guns and some bird guns made for shooting driven game set up with negative pitch. This is very rare and only done for specific situations.

The most important reason to adjust pitch is comfort. The proper pitch lays the butt of the gun flat into the shoulder, which allows the recoil to dissipate more evenly. The result is less felt recoil when the gun is fired. A flat-chested shooter may need +3 degrees of pitch to allow the butt of the gun to lay properly on the shoulder. However, a barrel-chested shooter would certainly need more positive pitch. A good fit for the average woman would be +6 degrees of pitch.

Be aware that pitch can have an effect on the elevation of the shot pattern. A butt stock with not enough positive pitch will tend to shoot high. If the toe is extended out too much in relation to the barrels, it can cause a slight elevation in the shot pattern. In general, a shotgun with negative pitch will tend to shoot higher than a gun with positive pitch.

Be aware that pitch and length of pull have an effect on each other. The proper length of a shotgun includes the correct pitch on the butt stock. When adjusting the length of pull, one should always consider the proper pitch on the butt stock. This will result in a more accurate and comfortable shotgun.

The pitch should create a comfortable angle for the butt of the gun to rest on the upper chest.

31

"Drop" yourself into the right stock

DROP, OR BEND AS IT IS OFTEN CALLED IN ENGLAND, essentially controls how high or low the shotgun will pattern. Drop is the distance from the top line on the comb to the rib on the barrels. Drop is measured in two key areas: at comb and at heel. The cheek should come to rest slightly forward of the middle point between these two measurements. Where the cheek lands on the stock is sometimes called drop at face.

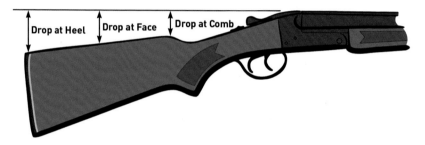

Drop at comb and, to a lesser extent, drop at heel control the elevation of your shot pattern.

Gun fitters typically do not use drop at face as a measuring point because there's no realistic need to measure it. Also, shooters tend to mount the gun at slightly different points atop the comb. This means that drop at comb and drop at heel create a better way to accurately measure drop.

Drop is important to the gun fitting process because it controls how high the eye will be relative to the rib or barrel, which means that drop dictates how high or low your gun will shoot. If your eye rests too high over the rib, your gun will pattern high. Sometimes this can be an advantage, and some stocks are purposely built this way. Most upland bird guns are built to pattern a touch high because flushed birds are often rising as the hunter takes the shot. This creates a degree of built-in lead, which is an advantage in certain situations. Most guns built exclusively for shooting driven birds have very little drop to them. This helps a shooter on high, incoming targets because the gun patterns high.

This gun clearly has too much drop for this shooter.

This gun does not have enough drop for this shooter.

This gun appears to have the proper amount of drop for this shooter.

Some older guns are built with excessive drop in the stock, creating tricky situations for the shooter. It is almost impossible to accurately shoot a gun that has too much drop. The eye simply cannot line up with the rib and the barrel. The shooter often finds himself looking into the back of the receiver. As a result, the off eye takes over and the miss is usually low and wildly left. Many shooters come to a shooting school and are mystified as to why they can't shoot their grandad's old shotgun. After measuring the drop and seeing them mount the gun, it often becomes clear why they are having so much trouble shooting the family heirloom.

The master eye simply can't see the rib or bead on the barrels. To shoot this gun accurately, they are forced to develop bad habits in their gun mount. For example, the gun is not fully pressed into the cheek during the mount, which is the only way the master eye can peer down the rib. Over time, they can learn to shoot such a shotgun, but when they switch to another gun, they often miss everything high.

Most modern shotguns are made with a length of pull near 14½ inches. The drop at comb is 1½ inches and the drop at heel is 2¼ inches. Many older style double guns have drop measurements of 1¾ at the comb and 2¾ at the heel. This much drop is excessive by today's standards.

I prefer to fit a shooter with slightly less than an inch difference between drop and comb and drop at heel. So, 1½ by 2¼ would be ideal. This creates a gun that recoils less and is more comfortable to point and shoot.

Stock design has a profound effect on how well a shotgun will fit you. Take the time to understand how drop affects your mount and patterns, and you will become a better shooter.

32

The proof is in the pattern

AS A RULE, MOST SHOTGUNS SHOULD PATTERN ABOUT 60/40. This means, on the patterning board, 60 percent of the pellets cover the target high and 40 percent cover it low. This is the classic setup for the upland bird hunter and makes sense because most upland birds flush off the ground and rise upward. A pattern that hits a little high helps the upland shooter connect on those rising birds and gives him a bit of built-in lead. Also, this allows the shooter to keep a visual connection with the target as the gun is fully mounted. The eyes can still see the target as the gun comes to the cheek and shoulder. The pattern covers the bird, but the eyes never have to be blocked out by the barrels.

If a gun patterns 40/60 low, it would be difficult for the shooter to see the bird and still hit it. When a gun patterns low, the shooter needs to block out the bird with the barrel as it rises. This blocking action may be necessary to hit rising targets. This is not desirable because the shooter loses visual connection with the target.

What happens if the bird swerves just as the gun mount is completed? One of the most important rules of successful shotgunning is that you must maintain intense visual concentration on the bird, particularly at the instant the trigger is pulled. A low-patterning gun makes it hard to maintain visual contact with the target.

Some clay shooters prefer a flatter pattern in their shotgun. A round of sporting clays may include many different target presentations. Some targets may be crossing and others may drop precipitously. A flatter pattern that is 50/50 is considered "neutral," allowing the shooter to react accordingly to the target.

The drop mostly dictates how the eye rests on the comb relative to the rib or top line of the barrels. Specifically, drop at comb has the greatest effect on the elevation of the shot. If the eye sits very high over the rib, the gun will pattern high. If the eye rests lower on the comb and rib, the gun will tend to shoot lower.

Typically, if a shooter aims down the barrel and can see the bead and the whole rib, the gun will pattern higher. As the shooter peers down the barrel and sees only the bead, the gun should pattern much flatter. If the shooter can't even see the bead in the mounted position, then the gun has too much drop. Ideally a shooter would like to see the bead and a little of the rib once the gun is fully mounted. Always take the time to pattern your shot gun to see how high or low the point of impact is.

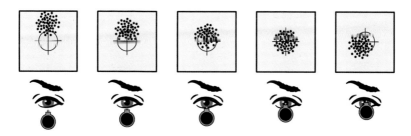

This is a general idea of how the gun will pattern depending on the eye and barrel relationship.

33

Cast off your misses to the right

DROP CONTROLS YOUR PATTERN HIGH AND LOW; NOW think of cast as directing the pattern to the left or right. Cast and drop have the most direct effect on the point of impact of the shotgun pattern. Even slight adjustments in cast or drop can have a profound effect on how your shotgun will pattern. Of all the elements in gun fitting, these are by far the most important.

Cast is the slight bend in the stock to the left or right in relation to the barrels or rib. This is designed to allow the focusing eye to be centered over the rib. Cast *off* is for the right-handed shooter, and cast *on* is for the lefty.

The key to gun fitting is to ensure that the gun shoots where the shooter's eyes are focused. A right-handed shooter handling a gun without cast will usually find it patterning a touch to the left. This is fine on targets going right to left, but on other presentations, it can cause misses. If the eye lines up slightly left on the rib, then the gun will shoot somewhat to the left.

Cast simply allows the dominant eye to be centered on the barrels. If the eye and barrels line up, the gun will shoot wherever the eye is focused.

Any shooter can use a little cast bent into the stock. How much can depend on the shape of the shooter's face and fullness of his cheeks. Another factor is the set of the eyes. Are the eyes close together or far apart? Even the slope of the shoulders or the thickness of the stock can affect cast. A very thick comb may result in the pattern going left or right. The opposite holds true with a gun that has a very thin comb. Less cast would need to be bent into a stock with a very thin comb.

Also, adjustments for cast should be made in small increments. Almost every right-handed shooter could use $\frac{1}{8}$ inch of cast off. However, it's rare that a shooter would benefit from more than $\frac{3}{8}$ inch of cast.

Side-by-side shotguns tend to need more cast, but on single-barrels or over-unders, cast should be doled out carefully. The reason is simple: We don't want to bend the stock too much away from the center line of the barrels. If the cast is excessive, the gun will feel clumsy and awkward. Also, a gun with excessive cast will produce more felt recoil.

If your shotgun is patterning left or right, the proper amount of cast can put your pattern back on target!

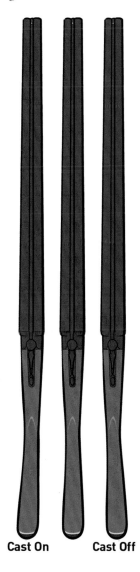

Cast On   **Cast Off**

This image illustrates the two types of cast. Cast off is for right-handed shooters, and cast on is for left-handed shooters.

34

Check the measurements of your stock

IT'S A USEFUL EXERCISE TO MEASURE YOUR SHOTGUN'S stock for gun fit. The professional gun fitter often uses a drop stick to determine the key components of gun fit. A drop stick can quickly measure drop at comb and drop at heel. Some drop sticks can also measure cast.

No need to worry if you don't have access to a drop stick. You can discover everything you need to know about your gun stock with a tape measure, ruler, and table.

For length of pull, measure from the center of the trigger to the middle of the butt stock. This measurement is called length of pull. Most standard shotguns will measure from fourteen inches to 14¾ inches. Any longer or shorter means the stock may have been altered at some point.

Next, take a measurement of the drop. Simply place the gun upside down so that the rib rests securely on a table top, with the bead hanging over the edge of the table. This will ensure that the barrel is lying flat. Measure the drop at comb by reading the distance from the comb to the table. The average off-the-rack shotgun will measure 1½ at the comb. Do the same to ascertain drop at heel. Typically, drop at heel will be 2¼ to 2½ inches.

To measure pitch, find the twenty-six-inch mark on the barrels. Start where the barrel begins. Place a piece of tape on the rib at the twenty-six-inch mark. Next, place the shotgun against the wall so that the butt of the gun is flush with the floor. The receiver of the gun should be touching the wall, and the barrels should be sticking out slightly. Now, simply measure the distance from the twenty-six-inch mark on the barrels to the wall. Every ½ inch will equal one degree of pitch. So, if the measurement is two inches, the butt has +4 degrees of pitch. If the measurement is three inches from the wall, the butt has +6 degrees of pitch.

Measuring your own stock can be very useful. If you have been fit for a set of dimensions with a Try Gun, you can compare and contrast

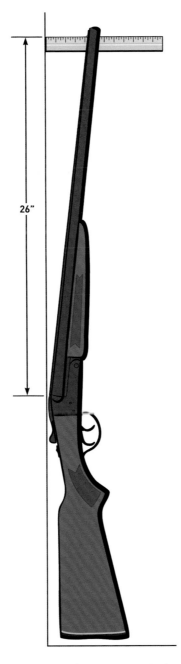

26"

Pitch can be measured in inches at the twenty-six-inch mark of the barrels.

those numbers with your own shotgun. Also, with practice you will begin to understand which stock dimensions are most comfortable for you. I know there are certain stock dimensions that I simply can't shoot. I wouldn't buy a gun with stock dimensions that I wasn't 100 percent comfortable with.

35

Before you buy, consider a bespoke gun

I KNOW SOME PEOPLE ARE READING THIS AND ROLLING their eyes. In their heads, they are saying, "Me? Buy a custom-made shotgun? Are you crazy?"

The benefits of the fitted gun are numerous. I've performed thousands of fittings in my many years as an instructor, and I've seen the benefits firsthand. It's imperative that your gun fit you properly if you want to shoot your very best. One of the most important keys to successful shooting is that the gun shoots where your eyes are looking. This is only achieved if the gun fits correctly.

Many shooters can pick any gun off the rack and learn to handle it reasonably well. This is especially true if you are of average build and height. After all, most guns are built to fit the average person. But what if you're not average? This is where shooting problems begin.

Many shooters bring a gun to a shooting school only to find that the gun they are trying to learn with does not fit them very well. Learning to shoot with an ill-fitting shotgun can be frustrating, and missing targets repeatedly can be infuriating.

During a lesson, I may ask a student to try another gun because I know the gun he is using is causing him to miss. Reluctantly, he will give up the gun and try one with a better fit. Often, I don't even have to change the way he is shooting. After a few shots, he starts busting clays with ease. It is quite a revelation to find that even though you have the ability to break the target, your own shotgun is holding you back.

Learning to shoot with a gun that doesn't fit frequently results in the development of bad habits. The student now has to break those bad habits in order to shoot effectively. It's much easier to develop proper form right from the start than it is to break bad habits later on.

Which brings us to the benefits of a custom-fitted shotgun. Many students who come to the Orvis Shooting School discover that their own shotguns don't fit them. They usually end up selling those guns and buying a gun that is better suited for them. Wouldn't it have been cheaper to start with a properly fitted shotgun?

This is not to say you should run out and buy a matched pair of the most expensive custom-made shotguns. You can find reasonably priced models with dimensions tailored to your physique.

I advise students to pay attention to the wood, not the metal. Often, we are seduced by fine engraving, etching, and inlays. The silver and gold catches the eye, and we imagine ourselves hunting quail in Georgia with a sweet new twenty-eight-gauge double. However, it is only the stock that can be customized to fit the owner.

Most gun makers offer some degree of stock adjustment in their base model shotguns. If you are looking to keep costs down, avoid the fancy engraving and spend your money on a perfectly-fitted stock. Many companies will offer the fitting service at no charge when you are buying a bespoke (custom) shotgun.

I encourage every shooter to consider having a stock tailored to his personal dimensions. A custom gun is not much more expensive than many off-the-rack shotguns. Isn't the goal to enjoy shooting more?

Before you buy a shotgun, get fit and consider a bespoke gun.

PART

VI

Parts of a Shotgun

36

Learn your shotgun's safety features

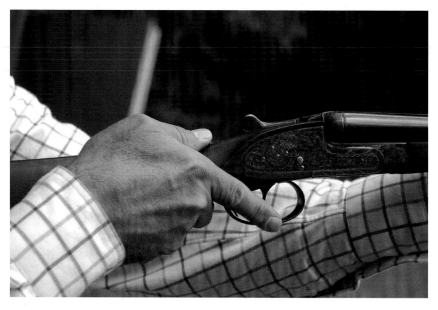

Learn the proper operation and timing of your gun's safety.

IT IS IMPORTANT THAT EVERY SHOOTER UNDERSTANDS THE proper operation and function of the shotgun safety mechanism. In the "On" position, the safety is designed to prevent the trigger from being pulled. However, any safety mechanism is prone to failure. As an added precaution, never touch the trigger until you are ready to shoot the gun.

There are two types of safeties: the manual safety and the field safety. The manual safety (standard on most repeating shotguns) is always on or off. In order to have the safety block the trigger from firing the gun, the shooter must manually move the safety to the On position. When the safety button is moved into the Off position, it will stay there until the shooter moves it back to the On position. Most sporting clays, autos, and pump shotguns have this type of safety.

A field safety is found on many break-action shotguns. This means that every time the barrel and action are completely broken open, the safety automatically clicks back into the On position. This added safety feature built into field guns makes sense. The action can be fast and furious in the field. This function means that the shooter does not to have to manually reset the safety after reloading the gun. Every time a shooter takes a shot and breaks open the gun, the safety is automatically returned to the On position.

It is important to understand when to disengage the safety while shooting. Make disengaging the safety part of your gun mount. When you begin to engage the target, you can switch off the safety. Once the butt of the gun comes out from below the armpit, the safety may be disengaged. Seasoned shooters learn to automatically flip the safety back on if the shot is not taken. It simply becomes second nature.

37

A shotgun shooter never squeezes the trigger

A SHOTGUN'S TRIGGER IS A SENSITIVE MECHANISM. THE trigger finger should be placed on the trigger only when the shooter is ready to fire the gun. In rifle shooting, it's standard procedure to slowly squeeze the trigger. The shotgun shooter touches the trigger only when the shot is ready to be taken.

The trigger finger should rest alongside the trigger guard at all times until the shooter is ready to fire the gun. Many shooters accidentally pull the trigger before they are ready to take the shot. Some are barely in the ready position when the gun goes off.

Often, a shooter will fire the gun accidentally when pushing off the safety. This usually occurs when the index finger is touching the trigger. The thumb pushes the safety, and the finger naturally pulls for leverage, and . . . *boom!* This is not what we want to see in the field or at the range.

The index finger should remain outside of the trigger guard during the swing and mount. Once the gun is completely mounted to the shoulder and cheek, the index finger can pull the trigger. It takes only a fraction of a second to touch the trigger correctly. No time will be lost by keeping the finger on the trigger guard.

The trigger pull refers to how much pressure it takes to fire the gun when the trigger is pulled. This is typically set by the manufacturer. Some clay shooters prefer a lighter trigger pull, but most field guns are set with heavier trigger pulls. The standard rule is that the weight of the trigger pull is set at about half the weight of the gun. So, if the gun weighs seven pounds, the trigger is set at 3½ pounds. Some shotguns have adjustable triggers that vary from a few ounces to four pounds or more.

Remember that the shotgun shooter touches the trigger only when he is ready to fire the gun. This is proper shooting form and makes for safer days afield.

The finger should rest along trigger guard while the thumb pulls off the safety.

The tip of the pointer finger touches the trigger only when the shooter is ready to fire.

shorter length of pull when selecting a pistol grip–style gun. The difference is typically ¼ inch. A shooter fit for a straight grip that's around 14¾ inches may only need 14½ inches when shooting a pistol-grip stock.

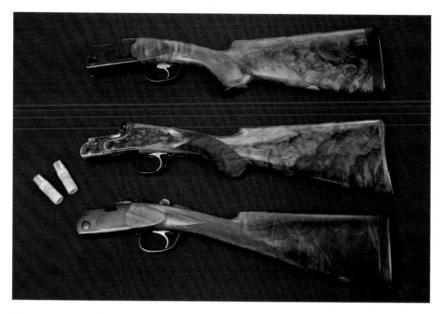

There are many different grip styles to consider.

40

Barrel length and its effect on shooting

BARREL LENGTH IS OFTEN OVERLOOKED WHEN SELECTING a shotgun, but it can have a tremendous impact on a shooter's ability to hit a target.

The upland hunter tends to prefer shorter barrels, especially in thick cover.

How long should the barrels be on a shotgun? That depends on several factors.

Let's start with field guns. Most eastern bird hunters tend to favor short-barreled shotguns, which tend to be lighter and easier to handle when trudging through typically thick upland cover. These shooters want a light-weight, fast-pointing gun with a shorter barrel.

The sporting-clays shooter may favor slightly longer barrels. Longer barrels tend to swing more fluidly on long passing shots. They add more weight to the muzzle for a smoother swing, which can be helpful on longer crossing and incoming clay presentations. The bird hunter who does a lot of pass shooting on sea ducks or doves may also find longer barrels better at swinging on the target. Barrel length can depend greatly on what the gun was designed to do.

Another consideration is the length of pull. I always tell shooters I fit that the barrel length should complement the length of pull. So, if a shooter has a fifteen-inch length of pull, longer barrels will help balance the overall feel of the gun. I don't think I would ever recommend twenty-six-inch barrels on a gun with a stock length of 15¼ inches. Conversely, if a shooter has a 13¾-inch length of pull, longer barrels may make the gun too "muzzle heavy."

I prefer longer barrels on my shotguns. I have long arms and a length of pull around 14¾ inches. I don't feel comfortable shooting anything shorter than a gun with barrels that are less than twenty-eight inches. Short-barreled guns feel whippy and unbalanced to me. Many shooters consider anything longer than twenty-eight inches as too long.

Sporting clay shooters often favor slightly longer barrels.

41

The pros and cons of shotgun ribs

THE RIB ON A SHOTGUN SITS ATOP THE BARREL. ITS function is to help the eyes align with the end of the muzzle. However, in practice, the rib should have very little effect on shooting performance. Many tips in this book have emphasized the need for unwavering focus on the target. You almost never hear a shooter say, "Man, good thing I had the rib and my eye lined up when I took that shot." If a shooter spent time trying to line up the eye and rib during a shot, I guarantee the result would be a miss.

A rib should be a minimally intrusive feature on the barrel. This is especially true for the wingshooter. Most field guns have low-profile ribs that do not distract the shooter. This keeps the hunter's focus on the flushing bird and allows him or her to pull the trigger at the right moment without distraction.

Some sporting clay guns have a raised rib with a high profile. A raised rib effectively lowers the shot pattern. Clay shooters tend to prefer a flatter-shooting gun, so this makes perfect sense. A raised rib would seem to be more distracting, but the clay shooter has ample time to prepare for the target. When you know from when and where the target is coming, you heighten your focus in preparation for the shot. So, in a situation like this, a more intrusive rib may be less of a distraction.

If your gun fits you, the eye and the barrel will be in perfect alignment. Avoid a rib that is a distraction. It will only take your attention and focus away from the target.

42

The benefits of a small, low-profile bead

MANY TIMES, A CLIENT WILL ATTEND AN ORVIS SHOOTING School and claim he simply can't shoot a shotgun. He has a hunting background, but he has mostly hunted with rifles.

One feature these folks like to put on their gun is a big glow-in-the-dark bar or bead, right on the end of the barrel. On seeing this, our team of instructors knows what the problem is. We can tell right off the bat who the rifle shooters are.

Most rifle shooters tend to aim at a target the moment they pull the trigger. A good instructor will know when a shooter is aiming his gun. The gun barrels come to a stop, and the swing is aborted. Once a shooter's eye locks in on the bead, the barrels tend to come to a screeching halt. The focus on the target is lost, and the miss is typically behind the clay.

Even the most experienced rifle shooter can learn to keep his focus on the target as he pulls the trigger. One of the first things we do for the rifle shooter is take the bead off of the gun. At first, these shooters seem lost; however, once they start busting targets, they begin to see that the glowing distraction on the end of the gun was holding them back.

The bead may be the most useless part of the gun. After a few misses, a shooter will subconsciously start aiming. This is natural. After a miss or two, the shooter begins to think, "Where am I missing"? On the next shot, the eye struggles to see where the barrel is in relation to the target. The focus is taken away from the bird, and the shooter misses again. The shooter simply needs to heighten his focus on the target and ignore the barrels. This may be counterintuitive, but on a miss, the shooter needs to ignore the end of the gun and direct his focus to the target. If there is a bead on a shotgun, it should be low-profile and not distracting to the shooter.

A low-profile bead is less distracting and allows a shooter to keep his eyes on the target.

43

Where to place the lead hand

THE FOREND IS THE SMALLER PIECE OF WOOD IN FRONT OF the action. Some forends are big and bulky; others are thin and have a low profile. Often, the forend is quite long, providing room to slide the pointing hand forward or backward depending on the shooter's physique.

At the Orvis Shooting Schools, we teach the instinctive method of shooting based on several English methods or styles. One of the fundamentals of the Orvis Method is that the lead hand controls the pointing action of the gun. The lead hand points or swings in concert with the bird as the gun is raised to the shoulder and cheek. Pointing and swinging become one harmonious movement. The lead hand functions best if the arm is held nearly straight.

Here's a simple test. Point at a songbird flying through the air. When you do this, you will notice that your arm is nearly straight. This is exactly how the pointing hand should function when swinging on a moving target.

Experiment where you hold the lead hand on the forend. Most shooters find that they can track the target's path better with the lead hand extended on the forend.

Sometimes, it's a benefit to move the hand back slightly while gripping the forend. For example, when you are hunting ducks, you may have several layers of clothing on and your gun seems a bit long. By moving the lead hand back, you can draw the gun out a bit farther. This can help make it easier to complete the gun mount.

Be aware that allowing the lead hand to creep back too far on the forend can lead to a seesaw-type gun mount. This is when the hands work independently and the barrels dip off the line of the target.

As a general rule, it's best to extend the lead hand out on the forend. This will allow the hands to work in unison, and you'll keep the barrels on target.

Use the forend only as a suggestion as to where to place the lead hand.

44

Understand how choke affects the shot string

CHOKE IS THE RESTRICTION AT THE END OF THE BARREL that controls how the shot string spreads out over a given distance. There is an effective range that a shotgun can reach and still cleanly kill a bird or break a clay target. Choke helps a shooter dial in this range and depends greatly on what type of shooting you may be doing. For example, the clay shooter might need a different shot pattern than a duck hunter at forty yards. For one, the clay shooter needs only one pellet to break a brittle clay target, whereas the duck hunter needs more (and bigger) pellets to take down a mallard at thirty-five or forty yards.

The choke helps control how the shot string opens up over a given distance. A tighter choke will hold the string together longer, and a more open choke will spread the pellets out faster.

There are four basic chokes: cylinder, improved cylinder, modified, and full. The most open choke is cylinder; the most restrictive choke is full. Cylinder opens the shot pattern to a forty-inch spread at about twenty-five yards. Improved cylinder opens up to a forty-inch spread at about thirty yards. Modified choke opens up a forty-inch spread at about thirty-five yards. And lastly, full choke opens up a forty-inch spread at approximately forty yards. These numbers can vary a bit depending on load and pellet size.

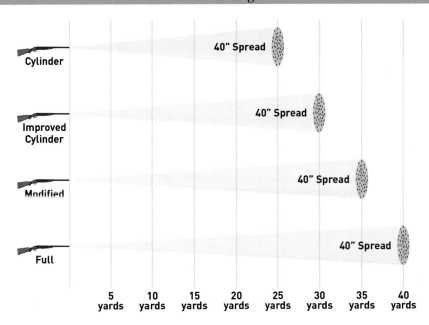

Cylinder   40" Spread

Improved
Cylinder   40" Spread

Modified   40" Spread

Full   40" Spread

5   10   15   20   25   30   35   40
yards   yards   yards   yards   yards   yards   yards   yards

Understand how choke affects the shot string.

45

Choosing the proper recoil pad

SOME GUNS HAVE WOOD BUTTS AND OTHERS HAVE RECOIL pads installed on the end of the stock.

Recoil pads are often put on a butt after the stock has been shortened or lengthened. It's an easy way to change the length of pull without having to build a new stock. A quality recoil pad can be more comfortable to shoot compared to a stock with a wood butt. Truthfully, the reduction of recoil is minimal when you add a recoil pad to a gun. However, a recoil pad can adjust the pitch, which can alleviate the felt recoil on the shoulder. Also, a properly installed recoil pad will stay in place better once it is fully mounted to the shoulder pocket.

Often, recoil pads are constructed out of rubber, but they are very difficult to slide into the mounted position. Rubber holds in place very well, but it often gets hung up on clothing as the shooter tries to mount the gun. Rubber recoil pads work best for shooters who pre-mount the gun. Many trap guns have rubber butt pads on the stock. Rubber recoil pads are not suited for the bird hunter or clay target shooter who mounts and shoots quickly from the low gun-ready position.

I keep a roll of electrical tape in my shooting bag and use it to cover my students' rubber recoil pads. I can make a decent electrical tape cover for those sticky rubber recoil pads. This is a quick and simple fix and stops the rubber recoil pad from hanging up on a student's shirt.

Leather-covered recoil pads are another option. Leather slides up from a low gun-ready position without hanging up on a shooter's vest or clothing. Also, leather holds well in the shoulder once the gun is mounted. If your gun has a recoil pad, be sure that it's made from the proper materials.

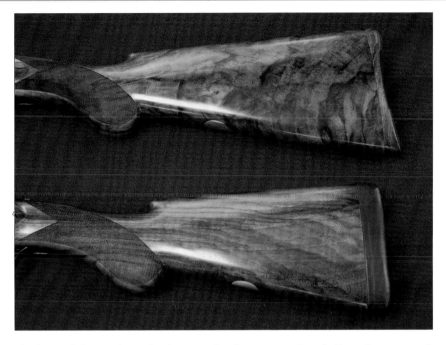

The butt of the stock can be just wood or have a recoil pad. If you have a recoil pad, leather is preferred.

Clay-Target Shooting

46

Sporting clays—the wingshooter's preseason

Shooting clay targets can be an excellent way to prepare for the bird-hunting season.

ANY BIRD HUNTER SHOULD SHOOT CLAY TARGETS during the off season to develop or hone his shooting skills. Every serious bird hunter looks forward to October—leaves changing color and crisp autumn mornings. However, before fall birds can be pursued, there is some preparation required. The waterfowler sorts through his decoys and brushes out his hunting blinds. The upland hunter cleans out his vest and tries to get the dog in shape by taking long walks in the woods.

The wingshooter should also set time aside to practice his technique. There is nothing worse than missing that first opening-day grouse and getting the cold shoulder from the dog. Clay target shooting, specifically sporting clays, is intended to mimic common bird-hunting situations. It's an ideal preseason warm-up for hunters.

For added realism, always shoot from a low-gun, ready position. Many games like skeet and trap are often shot with a pre-mounted shotgun. This means that the gun is placed into the shoulder and cheek before the shooter calls, "Pull!" Even though this is a fine way to break targets, it's not a realistic approach for the wingshooter.

Whenever possible, the wingshooter should swing and mount the gun just as he would in the field.

47

Shoot instinctively on the basic going–away target

SOMETIMES WHEN SHOOTING CLAYS, THE MOST BASIC target can give shooters fits. For example, why is it that we miss the easy going-away target? Often, it's a question of focus, and sometimes it's a question of technique. The truly straightaway target can be tricky. It's more difficult to pick up the flight line of the target when its path is straight away. A crossing target, for example, is much easier to track than the clay that is flying straight into the sky. A clay shooter can track the line of a crossing target with the pointer finger in practice before calling pull. He knows where the target is coming from and where it is going. The line of flight is much harder to track on a straightaway target.

I train my shooters to focus on the target and react instinctively once the clay is launched. One trick I use to have shooters be more instinctive is to have them *not* call pull. I will launch the clay at random. This way, the shooter simply reacts to the flight of the bird. The sudden surprise of the target flying into the air makes the shooter react more naturally. When he's allowed to call for the target, the shooter is anticipating its flight. When this happens, the eye and hands are out of sync.

To solve this problem, I tell my shooters to look for some small detail on the clay. On a straightaway target, I often tell them to look at the rings atop the clay. When they focus on the target, the result is usually dramatic: The clay is powdered into a cloud of orange smoke. The center of the shot string covers the clay completely, and the target is obliterated. The look on the shooters' faces is priceless: They light up when they realize how focusing on a minor detail on the clay can up their score. They may focus on the leading edge of the clay or the twelve o'clock position. Whatever the detail, it should narrow the shooters' focus down to a very small point.

This narrow focus also makes the shooters react more instinctively. The eyes pick up the detail and the body simply reacts more naturally due to the heightened concentration. Work on shooting the easy targets instinctively, gradually working your way to the more difficult targets. This should train you to keep your focus sharp, so that you can break more targets.

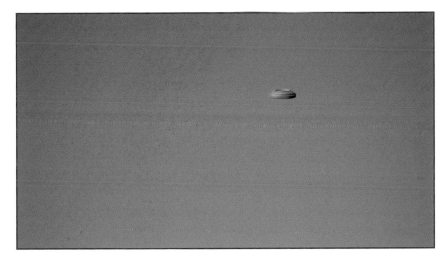

On a straightaway target, look for some detail on the clay like the rings. Often, this heightens focus and lets the shooter become more instinctive.

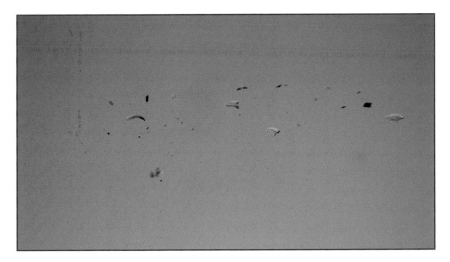

The results are often a solid hit.

48

Blocking out an incoming target

THE HIGH, INCOMING TARGET CAN BE A CHALLENGING shot. For one thing, the bird is flying directly at you. On most other clay target presentations, the bird is flying away from the shooting stand. If you take your time and don't rush the mount, this target becomes easier. The clay will fly into effective shooting range if you are patient.

Barrel movement is the key for most shooters. Learn to block out the target with the barrel before pulling the trigger.

It works like this: As the target is launched, the shooter picks up the incoming clay with his eyes. Smoothly, the gun is lifted up from the ready position. The lead hand begins to draw the gun into the path of the bird. As the clay flies into range, the gun is fully mounted. This part is the key. Once the gun mount is finished, the lead hand draws the barrels ahead of the bird, momentarily blocking out the target with the muzzle. I know I've said time and again to focus on the bird, but this technique is fun to try. The only way to lead this target is to cover it with the barrel.

Some shooters find it helpful to block out the incoming target with the barrels.

A shooter will often pull the trigger once the muzzle blocks the target from view. This can be helpful. The shooter instinctively knows that once the target is covered, it is time to pull the trigger. Other shooters prefer to come up from behind and overtake the incomer. This is when the shooter mounts the gun with the eyes on the tail of the clay and then draws ahead of it, blocking out the target. This slight swinging through the clay makes it easier to establish the proper lead and block out the target with the barrels.

Blocking out the incomer works best when the shooter closes the off eye as he mounts the gun. It can still be effective if done with both eyes open, but if you have trouble with this shot, consider closing the off eye.

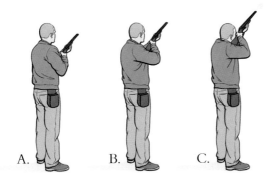

A.   B.   C.

A: The shooter begins in a proper ready position and picks up the bird with the eyes.
B: The gun is smoothly raised up as the front hand tracks the bird from behind to ahead.
C: The gun mount is completed and the barrels are drawn ahead, blocking out the incoming target.

49

How to "swing through" the right-to-left crosser

"SWING-THROUGH" IS ONE OF THE MOST EFFECTIVE WAYS to shoot a right-to-left crossing target. For the right-handed shooter, this is the most natural of the crossing shots. The gun is swung to the left with the left hand pulling the gun to its side of the body. For some reason, it seems more natural for righties to swing the gun onto a right-to-left target.

Swing-through means pointing the barrels along the flight path of the bird. The pointing hand draws a line from the tail of the target until the eyes and barrels overtake the clay. In essence, you are swinging through the flight path of the target with the hands and eyes. This can be an effective quick movement because you have to double the speed of the target in order to get ahead of it. Once the eyes and barrel overtake the bird, the mount is completed and the shot is fired. The required amount of lead is instinctively built into the shot if the eyes remain focused on the target. (Refer to tip No. 15 on picturing your lead.)

When trying the swing-through technique, always swing and mount the gun in one smooth motion. The most common mistake is that shooters mount the gun to the shoulder and cheek too soon. The gun is yanked to the shoulder as soon as the shooter sees the bird. Then, the gun is swung wildly in a mad race to get ahead of the clay. If you shoulder the gun too soon, the gun barrel can obscure your view of the target's flight path. Raising the gun smoothly provides a clear view of the clay. Once the eyes and barrel swing ahead, finish the mount and pull the trigger.

Some shooters are tempted to aim with the barrels when they mount too soon. The longer you are in the mounted position, the more tempting it is to lock on to the end of the gun and try to aim.

Swinging through the target is best performed by blending the swing and mount in one seamless move. A seasoned clay shooter points the barrel along the fight path of the bird as the gun is smoothly raised to the shoulder and cheek.

Begin your swing with the lead hand. The pointing hand starts the swing only as the eyes pick up the flight of the clay. This will make for a smoother, more efficient mounting movement. If the grip hand starts the movement, the barrel often drifts off the bird's flight line and leads to a see-saw gun mount. The grip is lifted up, causing the barrels to dip. A smoother swing and mount occurs when the pointing hand initiates the movement of the gun.

A: The shooter sets up in a proper ready position with muzzle held just below the line of sight.

B: The shooter picks up the target with the eyes, and the lead hand begins the movement by drawing the gun onto the line of the target.

C: The gun is smoothly brought up to the shoulder and cheek as the lead hand and eyes swing ahead of the target.

D: The mount is completed and the shot is taken as the shooter swings ahead. The shooter should resist any temptation to aim the gun. The swing-through should be smooth and flowing if the eyes stay connected to the flight path of the target.

50

How to "pull away" from a left-to-right crosser

THE LEFT-TO-RIGHT CROSSING SHOT CAN BE A BIT MORE difficult for some shooters. One issue is gun fit. If a right-handed shooter is shooting a gun without cast, the shooter's pattern is most likely going to be to the left. Most off-the-rack shotguns have no cast bent into the stock. This means that on a left-to-right target, the shooter is at a disadvantage. A gun that patterns a touch left has a little built-in lead on a right-to-left crossing target. On a left-to-right target, most shooters miss behind the target. Also, the left-to-right shot is not a natural swing for most right-handed shooters. It's going against the grain for the pointing hand and the body. Shooters tend to drop the head during the mount on this type of shot, especially when their footwork is not spot on.

Frequently, shooters will try the swing-through technique on a left-to-right target and discover that they simply can't develop the proper lead picture. This happens for many of the reasons listed above. On a left-to-right crossing bird, a change of method can result in more consistent success.

When a student is having problems on this type of crossing shot, I will have him try the "pull-away" method. This is a little different from the swing-through move. In this technique, the shooter tries to avoid letting the target get ahead of the pointing hand and the muzzle. The shooter picks up the target with the eyes and then points the barrel right at the clay. As the gun is smoothly mounted, the eyes and gun stay focused on the target. As the gun is pressed into the mounted position, the shooter pulls ahead of the target, "pictures" the lead, and pulls the trigger. You track right with the target, but as the mount is completed, you simply pull ahead of the clay and pull the trigger.

Always picture the lead without measuring it with the gun barrel. The body and eyes naturally try to get out ahead of the target if you avoid trying to aim. When you toss a football to your buddy cutting across the lawn, you don't consciously think about where to throw the ball. You just look at him running and throw it out ahead. You don't stop to measure where the football needs to go. You get in your own way when you try to analyze rather than react to the situation.

One other detail to be mindful of is the setup on a left-to-right crossing shot. Poor setup and footwork put the body at a disadvantage in this type of presentation. Be sure that when you set up in the shooting cage, you place the lead foot slightly ahead of where you intend to bust the target. This allows the body a little more room to unwind. Pointing the lead foot slightly ahead of the kill zone promotes a better follow-through and keeps the head and shoulders steady as the shot is taken.

If the left-to-right shot is giving you fits, try the pull-away technique. You may find it easier to lead the target and subsequently break more clays.

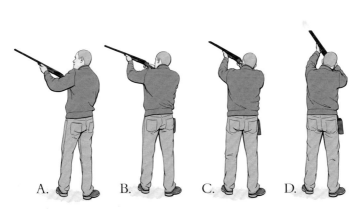

A: The shooter sets up up in a proper ready position. For the left-to-right shot, the lead foot should point more toward the break point as the upper body rotates back to pick up the target.
B: The shooter picks up the clay with his eyes, and the lead hand points the barrel right at the target.
C: The shooter points directly at the target as the gun comes up into the mounted position.
D: The gun mount is completed and the shooter deliberately "pulls" ahead of the target. Once the shooter pulls ahead, the shot is taken.

51

How to pick up the target

You can clearly see that the shooter's eyes and muzzle hold are downrange. This is so he can pick up the target when it first becomes a target and not a blur.

WHAT IS THE BEST WAY TO PICK UP THE TARGET? THIS IS A question I get all the time when coaching a new sporting clays shooter. Target presentation ultimately dictates where you should set your eyes to first pick up the target. Focus the eyes on the spot where the target first becomes clear and is not a blur. For example, you can see the trap house when the target comes flying out of. If you looked directly into the trap house, the target would appear to be a blur as it is launched out into the air. This makes it appear as if it were flying like a rocket. However, if you fixed your eyes a few yards away from the house, you would notice a point where the target comes into focus. Finding the spot where the target stops being

This allows the shooter to track the target with the eyes and point the gun more easily.

a blur allows the shooter to make a more effective reaction. The clearer you see the target, the smoother your reaction to it will be.

One of the advantages of sporting clays is that you are allowed to see the presentation before you even load the gun. This allows you to set up and consider the path of the clay. This is when you should pay close attention to where the target first becomes clear. More often than not, it's just a few yards from where the target first appears. If the eyes are looking directly at the spot where the target exits the chute, it appears as a blur.

Focusing on the point where the target is no longer a blur will give you a better look at the bird and allow you to smoothly react to the target's flight path.

52

Setup is a key fundamental to better clay shooting

MOST CLAY SHOOTING GAMES ALLOW YOU TO CALL FOR A target to be launched. In sporting clays, for example, you are even allowed a preview of the target presentation, which allows you to set up in the best possible position to attack the target.

This is different from most wingshooting situations. Wouldn't it be nice to call in some ducks by just saying "Pull!"?

Clay shooting affords the shooter the time to set up in the best position possible to break the target. The proper setup allows for the most efficient move possible. The setup can be particularly important on faster targets or when shooting doubles.

Let's start with a single.

The first thing to do is establish where your eyes can pick up the target clearly. Remember the previous tip: Look to see where the target transitions from a blur to a clean, round clay. Next, establish a break point. The break point is when you want to take the shot and bust the clay. As a general rule, this is at the apex of the target's flight path. At this point, the target is not falling or rising and has slowed considerably. This most often is the optimal spot to take the shot.

Once you've establish the break point, place your lead foot so that it's pointing slightly past it. This allows the shooter to follow through more easily. The shooter's weight naturally shifts onto the lead foot, and the swing and mount will be uninterrupted. Next, set the muzzle just below the line of sight and hold it about halfway between the break point and where it's possible to see the target clearly.

Where you hold the gun in the ready is often referred to as the "hold point." Many shooters prefer to hold the gun a little closer to the focal point, or where the eyes first see the target clearly. You can experiment with where you establish your hold point by holding the barrel far enough away from the focal point, so that the target doesn't jump ahead of you. Also, establish the hold point far enough away from the break point to allow room for an effective swing.

I always tell students to repeat this mantra: "Feet, muzzle, eyes." Set up in that order, they can effectively swing with the bird and make a clean shot. Remember, clay shooting affords the shooter time to prepare for the clay presentation. The correct setup will make it much easier to bust the target. After all, few things in life are more satisfying then seeing a clay target explode a moment after you pull the trigger.

The clay shooter is allowed time for a proper setup. The lead foot should point at or slightly past the break point. The eyes should be fixed on the spot where the target first becomes clear. The muzzle can be held slightly past where the eyes first pick up the target. Think feet, muzzles, eyes!

53

When shooting doubles, take the target you see first

WHEN TWO CLAY TARGETS ARE IN THE AIR AT THE SAME time, it's called a "true pair." These are fun presentations, but mastering this shot can scramble the brain. The most common question is, "Which one do I take first?" The simplest answer is that you engage the target your eyes pick up first.

However, clay course managers sometimes set up a "brain scramble" double, as I call them. This is a very tricky presentation during which the eye is drawn to one target while the other target gets away. Typically on a brain scramble, the shooter's eye is drawn to the easier of the two targets. This allows the second bird to fly out of range or drop to the ground. Sometimes, this is due to a well-placed tree or bush.

You can clearly see which target the shooter is going after first.

When you encounter a brain scramble, examine the pair and determine which one has the smallest window. Often, you are forced to engage the target you have less time to shoot.

Doubles can be fun to shoot, but they can also be frustrating. Analyze each pair carefully. The one you pick up first is the best one to go after. Also, examine the shooting windows and break points for each clay. You will most often find that you must take the one with the shortest window first.

54

Use open chokes and target loads for clay shooting

WHEN SETTING UP FOR A ROUND OF CLAY TARGETS, USE the most open choke possible and match it with a quality target load. Most target guns, and modern field guns for that matter, feature screw-in, interchangeable chokes. This allows a shooter to switch chokes according to the situation. Generally, the clay shooter should have the most open choke possible while maintaining an effective shot string. When should you change chokes? I'm not a big choke changer, but many shooters are better than I am, so it's OK to do so. I only consider changing my choke when the target distances get beyond forty or forty-five yards. Normally, I prefer an improved cylinder choke.

Skeet shooters almost always use a cylinder or skeet choke. The skeet setting is a slightly tighter choke than cylinder. For most clay target presentations, cylinder, skeet, and improved cylinder are fine. I've seen shooters break targets at fifty-plus yards with cylinder chokes. This isn't necessarily the most effective choke at fifty yards, but it can work. Today's modern barrels are simply amazing because the chambers, bores, chokes, and ammunition are so much more effective.

What about when shooting a double-barrel shotgun? Some shooters put the same choke in both barrels, whereas others use a combination of chokes because it can be helpful on doubles to have two different chokes. This is especially true when the second shot is considerably farther away than the first.

Remember that it takes only one or two pellets to break a clay bird. For this reason, target loads often have the smaller pellet sizes in them. This creates a dense shot pattern and improves the chances of blanketing the target with a swarm of shot. For example, twelve-gauge target loads will often contain No. 7½ shot, and a twenty-eight-gauge target load will typically contain No. 9s. Target loads are lighter than most field loads and have a reduced shot charge in them. This helps reduce recoil, making it possible to shoot fifty or even 100 rounds without much of a pounding.

Use more open chokes when clay shooting.

The result is often a busted clay.

Finally, the lighter loads and modern wads reduce the number of deformed pellets. This means that more pellets stay in the swarm, improving the shooter's chances of hitting the target.

Whenever possible, use open chokes and target loads when shooting clay targets. This will lead to more broken clays and fewer sore shoulders.

55

Etiquette and safety procedures at the shooting range

I BROUGHT A FRIEND TO ORVIS'S SANDANOA SHOOTING Grounds for a round of sporting clays. Sandanoa is a first-class shooting facility offering everything the shotgun enthusiast desires. This was the ideal place to take my friend shooting for the first time. This fellow was not an outdoorsmen or shooter, but he had an interest in learning to handle a shotgun. I found him a gun off the rack that fit him fairly well, and off we went.

Pretty soon, my partner wandered ahead of our group and was walking down the path to the next station. He was holding his gun in the closed position as if he were carrying a briefcase. Another group of shooters approached him along the path. Abruptly, the trap operator with the approaching group halted his shooters. He politely shouted to my friend, "Excuse me, sir! Could you break open your gun?"

At this point, I could see what was unfolding. My buddy didn't quite understand what the trap operator was asking him to do. After a second request, I yelled ahead: "Open your gun!" He finally understood and quickly opened the action.

My friend was a serious golfer and conscious of proper etiquette. I could see that he was mortified, knowing he had breached the rules of range safety and etiquette.

After the other group had passed, I calmed him down and said, "I don't think you'll carry your gun closed like that again, will you?" Red-faced and embarrassed, he agreed.

There are safety and etiquette rules to be followed whenever you are handling shotguns. One is to *always* treat a shotgun as if it were loaded. Also, never point a gun at anything you don't intend to shoot. If you have a break-action gun (double-barrel or over-under), be sure it is open whenever you are moving about the range grounds. This allows the other shooters to see that your gun is out of battery and inoperable. The gun should be closed only when it is in the rack or when you are shooting. If you a carry an automatic, leave the action open as a viewing courtesy to the other shooters around you.

Most shooting areas have a set of safety and etiquette rules posted on the grounds. It's good from to familiarize yourself with them before heading out to shoot.

It is clear to see that these shooters are walking with their guns open. Familiarize yourself with the etiquette and safety procedures at the shooting grounds.

Field Shooting

56

The ready position for upland hunting

IN UPLAND COVER, YOU SOON LEARN TO WALK AND HUNT, holding the shotgun in a safe position across the chest, with the barrels pointed to the sky. The stock hangs low near the hip. This is a safe way to walk through the woods, but it's a difficult position to shoot from. The barrels are held high and the stock low. From this position, it can be difficult to connect with a bird flushing from cover. The barrels are often hatchet-chopped downward as the bird is rising. This is not a good way to connect with a fast-disappearing bird.

On pointed birds, there is usually ample time to assume a ready position, lower the shotgun barrel slightly, and walk in as the dog holds point.

As the dog goes on point, you should adopt a ready position for the flush.

Even when hunting over a flushing dog, there is time to set up for the flush. Most flushing dogs give a clear indication when they are about to flush a bird: The tail beat quickens and the nose often dips toward the ground. With experience, you can learn to read a flushing dog's pre-flush signs. When the dog gets excited, it's time to set up for the shot.

The ready position begins with the barrel just below eye level. The gun is never slung across the chest, and the muzzle is directed straight out toward the anticipated line of fire.

A friend who is a hunting guide instructs his clients to set up this way every time they walk into the point. It's much safer for him as he works the dog in the middle, and it's much safer for his clients as they walk up to the birds.

Here, the hunter notices his flushing dog getting "birdy." This sign allows the shooter to set the gun in a proper ready position.

57

When hunting grouse, the pointing hand is key

THE RUFFED GROUSE RANKS AS ONE OF THE MOST difficult of all upland birds to shoot. Three shots per bird is considered expert, and few experts bag their limit on every outing. These birds seem to enjoy thwarting the hunter's best efforts, and they are very good at what they do!

To begin with, grouse live in the most inhospitable cover—places man and dog prefer to avoid. It's rarely possible to get a clear shot at a flying grouse. You point and shoot where the bird should be and hope for the best.

Also, the ruffed grouse are crafty game birds with a knack for putting a tree between themselves and the gun barrel. Ironically, they are not the fastest flying game bird—it just seems that way. They rely on their cunning, and use the trees to make a clean getaway.

Am I giving this bird, with its small brain, too much credit? Maybe, but when you've missed as many grouse as I have, it's easy to understand why many hunters call this bird the "wood devil." Spend a season in the grouse woods, and then we'll talk!

Most grouse are up and gone in under three seconds, which gives hunters a very small window of opportunity. The shooter just reacts quickly to the flush of the bird. The lead hand is key to faster shooting.

Hunters often say they "snap shoot" at grouse. This is when you simply snap the gun ahead of where you see the bird going. I never liked the idea of snap shooting. To me, this seems as if the shooter is snapping the gun to a point where he thinks the bird is going. This can work at times. However, it seems as if there is no real connection to the flight path of the bird. It's as if the shooter hopes the bird will fly into his shot string.

Instead, let the leading hand point the barrel onto the bird as the eye picks up the flush. This way, the eye and hand are working together. This will feel as if you are punching out with the lead hand. For many shooters, this can prove a little difficult at first. If you are right-handed and shoot off of the right shoulder, it's the left hand that points the gun. In this case, the shooter needs to have the left hand drive the action. For shooters who are right-hand dominant, this may take some practice. Try it on the range. You will see that faster shooting is truly a product of a dominant lead hand.

The lead, or pointing, hand can be the key to connecting with the elusive ruffed grouse.

58

Pick out one bird in the covey when hunting quail

BEING A NEW ENGLANDER, I DON'T HAVE A CHANCE TO hunt quail as often as I would like. Orvis has a shooting school on the Florida–Georgia border, so whenever I'm down South, I always line up a quail hunt. The first covey that flushes always gets my heart pumping. Seeing eight or ten birds busting from the brush takes a little getting used to. Most North Country upland hunters are used to one or two birds rising on a flush.

The covey flush is a unique hunting situation. It is distracting to see so many birds in the air at one time. The urgent beating of wings and the number of birds in the air at once can make it difficult to focus. How else can it be that a covey of birds can take to the air at fifteen yards and you can still miss with both barrels?

This is called flock shooting. You shoot at all the birds at once instead of taking them one at a time. The secret is simple: Focus on one bird at a time. Narrow your focus by looking for some detail on one particular bird. You will often connect when you focus on the white-streaked head of a single bird and nothing else.

Pick one bird in the covey. This is the bird you should commit to. Keep your eyes locked on it until it falls.

The temptation is to switch birds if you miss on the first shot. This most often leads to missing twice. It's better to stay on the same bird and try to down it with your second shot. If you connect on your first shot, simply find another bird and repeat the process. Don't worry about the rest of the covey.

At the Orvis School in Manchester, Vermont, we have set up a quail walk. This is a series of clay target traps set up along a trail. At the final station, we can launch six clays into the air at the same time. This creates a realistic covey flush and allows a shooter to practice picking out one target at a time. After several strolls down the quail walk, most shooters are routinely able to bust two clays out of the "covey."

Most of the time, the first bird that the eye picks up is the easiest bird to kill. This is the "honey bird." If you are hunting alone, this is the one to engage. However, when hunting with a partner, often both shooters take the honey bird. The more you hunt quail, the more you will react smoothly to the covey flush. After a while you will learn to pick your shots more effectively. Etiquette suggests that if you are walking in on the right side of the dog, the birds that flush to the right are yours.

Remember, when hunting quail avoid looking at the whole covey. Pick out one bird at a time before you swing on another.

Avoid looking at the whole covey flush. This hunter's success came from narrowing his focus and locking in on one bird. (Photo courtesy of Jay Cassell)

59

Pheasants—go for the ring

THE PHEASANT WAS IMPORTED FROM CHINA AND introduced to the Western states in the late 1800s. It continues to be a prized game bird wherever it is found. I remember flying in to Pierre, South Dakota, for the opening day of pheasant season and being amazed at how many gun cases I saw in baggage claim. The airport seemed overrun with bird hunters.

For a large upland bird, pheasants can be difficult to hunt. They are known to hold tight or flush wildly out of range. In the early season, they tend to hold tighter and seem to flush more slowly and loudly than many upland game birds. Their trademark, cackling flush can cause many shooters to rush the shot. A rushed, flustered shot does not allow the pattern to open up to its maximum effectiveness. If you shoot too early, the pattern is not much bigger than a softball. Also, when you rush the shot, the gun mount is often incomplete. This is a major cause of misses when shooting clays and live birds. It's better to wait out the flush with steady hands and eyes until the bird offers a clean shot at an ideal range.

Another detail that tends to throw hunters off is the long tail of the male. Because most states do not allow hunters to kill female birds, shooters must be able to identify each bird in flight before pulling the trigger. The hen, or female pheasant, is dull brown in color and has a shorter tail. The rooster, or male pheasant, is brightly colored and has a much longer tail. This longer tail can draw the shooter's eyes behind the bird and cause a miss.

Another prominent feature of the male bird is that is has a white ring around the neck (ring-necked pheasant, anyone?). This can be an excellent focal point as the bird takes flight. If a shooter is focused on the leading edge of a bird, there is a much greater chance that he will connect with it in flight. Avoid being distracted by the long tail and look for that white ring around the bird's neck.

Looking for some detail, like the white ring on the neck, can be helpful when hunting ring-necked pheasants.

60

When shooting ducks, let them get closer

DUCKS CAN BE SOME OF THE EASIEST BIRDS TO SHOOT, especially as they settle into the decoys. Decoying ducks is what every duck hunter dreams of. I love to see the flare of their wings and their dropping feet as they settle into the decoys. Unfortunately, ducks don't always come directly into a decoy spread, which can be frustrating. After a while, a shooter is tempted to take shots at birds that are out of range. Be patient and stay out of sight, and the ducks may circle around and settle in on the next pass.

Ducks can also be wary, especially late in the season when they become call and decoy shy. Even in the best of conditions, they can have a tendency to loop around the decoys and stay just out of shooting range. Ducks tend to circle a few times in order to drop altitude before committing to landing. It's important to read them as they fly overhead. The more you hunt, the better you will be at knowing if the ducks are wary or just taking one more look before landing.

On some days, they come right in on the final pass, and on others, they just won't commit. Learn to read the "body language" of the flock, and give the ducks time to make their final pass.

One of the biggest mistakes a hunter makes is shooting at ducks before they are in range. Just last season, I was sitting in my duck boat with one of my best hunting partners. It was a slow day, and the birds were scarce. The ducks we did see stayed just out of shooting range. As the morning sun got higher, our hopes began to sink. Some days it's just like that. Well, lo and behold, another gang of birds showed itself. I worked the call lightly so as to not scare them away. Slowly, they began to show signs of interest in our decoys. They made one loop around our spread, and then another. Suddenly I heard my partner say, "Let's take 'em!" He stood up and started firing away. I sat in my spot, dumbfounded. To me, those birds were way out of range. He emptied his gun and didn't even touch a feather. After missing, he sunk back down on his bucket with his eyes fixed to the deck of the boat.

"Sorry," he said, "I thought they were just in range."

I just looked away and laughed. I had done the same thing before, and I knew how he felt.

In all fairness to my duck-hunting partner, it can be difficult to judge when ducks are in range. For one, looking at birds against the backdrop of the open sky doesn't give you much depth perception. If you are hunting in flooded timber or along a river with lots of trees, it can be easier to judge distance. You can pick certain limbs and branches as reference points, or even use a rangefinder.

However, when hunting on open water or vast crop fields, it can be tough to judge distance. As in clay target shooting, it's best to focus on one detail of the incoming ducks. Many times, you can only shoot certain species of ducks as you near your limit. At this point, it's better to let them get into range, so that you can make a positive identification before you pull the trigger.

Another option is to figure out the distance from the blind to the decoys. If you set them up at thirty yards, you will know the ducks are in range as they settle into the spread of decoys.

It would be nice if the ducks always loved the sound of our calls as well as the look of our decoy spread. Unfortunately, this doesn't always happen so find a way to judge when they are in range for a more successful hunt.

Figure out the distance from your blind to your decoys, and you'll be able to tell when ducks are in range. (Photo courtesy of Jay Cassell)

61

The proper chokes for waterfowling

FOR MANY WATERFOWL HUNTING ENTHUSIASTS, NOTHING beats sitting in the blind at first light as the ducks are coming in. Because shots may vary from twenty yards to forty-five yards or more, it is important to set up your chokes properly to maximize the effectiveness of your pattern.

Choke selection depends largely on what type of duck hunting you are doing. If you are hunting flooded timber, shots will be much closer than if you were hunting ducks on open water. When the ducks are setting right into the decoys, they tend to be at close range (assuming you set out your decoy spread correctly). At other times, they may only be passing and not really committing to your location. Pass-shooting ducks can be a bit more challenging, and in this case, you might consider a tighter choke.

A modified choke is the universal choice for hunting waterfowl. This allows the shot string to open up to a forty-inch spread at about thirty-five yards. When pass-shooting ducks, some prefer a slightly tighter choke, such as improved-modified, light-full, or even a full.

Don't be afraid to change your choke if the birds aren't coming in exactly as you had hoped. A tighter pattern can give you a little extra range and more clean kills. A wounded bird can spoil a hunt, and waterfowl are among the toughest of all birds to kill. The dog often has to chase the bird down, and a diving duck can give a dog fits. On open water, you may have to chase after a cripple with the boat. Always attempt to hunt down crippled birds. It is the legal and ethical thing to do. Make every effort to find and retrieve cripples on land or water.

The proper choke can put more pellets in the bird, which leads to cleaner kills.

The proper chokes can lead to more downed birds when hunting waterfowl.

62

Always carry nontoxic shot when hunting waterfowl

BE SURE TO USE NONTOXIC SHELLS WHEN HUNTING waterfowl at all times. Federal regulations do not allow you to use or be in the possession of lead shot while hunting waterfowl. The penalties can be severe if you mistakenly leave a box of target loads in your bag.

There are some excellent nontoxic waterfowl loads available. Steel is one of the most common, but it can be the least effective, especially at extended range. Even though it is fast out of the muzzle, it has very poor down-range, knock-down power.

The best nontoxic shot is heavy but soft. Steel is very light and very hard, which is why it quickly loses its down-range kinetic energy. Heavier products such as tungsten and bismuth are popular high-performance non-toxic options. These materials are heavier and have more down-range, knock-down power.

Imagine playing baseball and being hit by a pitch. Would you feel a wiffle ball being thrown into your back more or a baseball? The heavier baseball would certainly do more damage.

Often, it is said that speed kills, but this is only part of the equation when it comes to shotgun shells. When it comes to nontoxic shot for waterfowl, shot size is the key to creating a lethal blow (refer to tip No. 20). The larger shot sizes carry more energy and, hence, do more damage.

The most effective waterfowl pellet sizes are No. 2s, 3s, and 4s. Some hunters may use No. 4s and even No. 5s on smaller ducks such as teal. However, for most duck hunting situations, No. 2s and 3s perform beautifully. Another point to remember is that larger shot sizes tend to hold the pattern better at longer distances. This is another reason to favor slightly larger shot.

Be sure to use nontoxic shot when hunting waterfowl.

63

Learn some fancy footwork for field shooting

UPLAND BIRDS MAKE THEIR LIVING BY SURPRISING hunters, usually with an enthusiastic flush that comes without warning. Even if you have a dog on point, the birds can flush in unexpected directions. This can challenge the wingshooter who does not have the proper shotgun setup and footwork. When the birds take wing wildly, the unprepared shooter is caught, well, flat-footed!

As is the case in clay target shooting, the hunter should set his lead foot so that it is pointing in the general direction he expects to shoot. This can be a challenge when hunting wild birds.

Let's say you are quail hunting and walking up to a dog on point. You happen to be on the left side of the dog. Your partner is on the right. The birds flush. Only one goes your way, but it is going hard left. Your lead foot is not pointing in the right direction now. What do you do?

You could calmly take another step and place your right foot in the direction the bird is going. This can be an effective way to take the shot, but only if the bird allows you the time to adjust to its flight. Also, taking a step creates additional head movement. It becomes difficult to focus on a bird if the shooter's head is moving about.

Another method is to learn some wingshooter's footwork. This footwork is based on the Churchill method. Robert Churchill was a famous English shooting instructor, who taught his students how to effectively shoot driven game while occupying a shooting station or "butt." This type of footwork trains the shooter to swing and mount over either foot.

When hunting from a butt, the shooter has the birds pushed to him by beaters. On a driven hunt, most shots are incoming overhead and left or right. When shooting driven game, the shooter may have to swing to the right on one shot and then left on the next. Churchill's method had the shooter stand fairly square to the direct overhead bird. If the bird came in to the right, the shooter would swing the body and pivot onto the right foot. However, if the bird came in on the left, the shooter would then swing and pivot onto the left foot.

To do this effectively, the shooter will need a fairly narrow stance. The heels should be six to eight inches apart, and the feet and body should be relatively square to the line of fire. This setup should allow the shooter to swing freely in either direction and still smoothly mount the gun.

This technique can be a very helpful to the upland hunter. Often, there is little or no time to adjust your footwork as the birds take flight. This wingshooter's footwork can also be very effective on ducks. Sometimes the birds come in overhead, which makes for a very tough shot off of the left foot, especially if the birds are moving to the right. In a boat or blind, it can be difficult to set up on the lead foot. In this case, you simply stand up and pivot onto the left foot and swing onto those pesky birds that insist on flying to the right.

Churchill's teachings are still relevant today. They can take some practice, but the determined gunner can learn to pivot onto either foot and still shoot effectively.

The wingshooter's footwork allows you to take the shot off of either foot. This can take some practice to learn but can be very useful at times.

64

Find your ideal field gun

Finding *your* ideal bird gun can be a fun and interesting process.

SOME SHOTGUNS ARE MADE TO BE TAKEN AFIELD AND others are not. The ideal field gun depends on the type of hunting you do. I have some general advice on what makes a gun ideal for bird hunting and, more importantly, what makes it ideal for you!

Let's begin with weight. Field grade guns are typically lighter in weight. This makes them easier to carry on a long afternoon of chasing pointing dogs. However, try not to get caught up in finding the lightest gun possible. I personally do not like shooting a gun if it's too light. Such shotguns feel whippy and cumbersome in my hands; some weight is actually good. A gun that's too light may not swing and follow through as nicely as a slightly heavier model.

It's important to consider how a gun will handle at a given weight. The grouse hunter who walks the hills for hours may prefer an ultra-light shotgun. He needs something that is feather light and quick to sling into action. The quail shooter who hunts on game preserves may walk less and shoot a lot more and, thus, may want a heavier gun that is smoother to swing and mount. Also, a slightly heavier gun may help to absorb some recoil, as light guns with hot field loads produce considerable recoil.

The stocks on traditional double-barrel field guns are typically straight-gripped, which helps cut down on weight. The theory behind straight-grip stocks is that they put the shooter's hands more in line with each other. This could result in a smoother point and mount.

I believe there is some merit to this theory. However, in my years as a shooting instructor, I believe most shooters mount the gun better using a semi-pistol grip. This is particularly true with new shooters who have not yet developed a consistent mount. The angle of the hand in a pistol or semi-pistol grip allows them to press the gun into the cheek more effectively. That being said, the straight-grip stock is certainly a traditional feature of the field-grade gun. Remember, we are trying to find *your* ideal field gun. If you are a new shooter, you may feel more comfortable with a semi-pistol grip stock on your field gun.

The ideal bird gun should have a safety that automatically comes back on when the action is broken open. This is known as a field safety. In the heat of action, when the birds are flushing and your partner is reloading his gun, it's comforting to know that his safety automatically turns back on.

The final consideration is barrel length. As a rule, field-grade guns tend to have shorter barrels, which cut weight and make them faster to point. You read it all the time: "The field gun should have twenty-six-inch barrels." Many field-grade guns do come with twenty-six-inch barrels, but *your* ideal field shotgun may not. Some shooters with longer pull lengths might want longer barrels to help balance the gun. If your length of pull is between 14¾ inches and fifteen inches, twenty-six-inch barrels may feel awkward. Also, a little more barrel weight produces a smoother swing gun on those tough crossing shots. Most shooters have a harder time pass-shooting birds with shorter barrels at longer distances. Again, it's all about what you intend to shoot with your ideal bird gun. To further complicate matters, the ideal woodcock gun may not be the ideal pheasant gun. Finding the perfect field gun can be a fun and interesting journey. And, you may need to buy more than one!

65

The correct chokes and loads for upland shooting

UPLAND HUNTING IS THE CRAFT OF WALKING UP ON GAME birds. The upland hunter typically uses a dog to help locate birds. The birds are then flushed off the ground into the air, and the hunter tries to take them down with an effective shot. In an ideal situation, the birds hold tight, and the shooting is at relatively close range. Most upland hunters who use double-barrel shotguns set up with improved cylinder and modified chokes. This provides a more open pattern on the first shot, and as the birds fly away, there is a slightly tighter choke for the second.

Unfortunately, the birds don't always hold tight and flush at twenty yards. Toward the end of the hunting season, birds may flush a little farther out after weeks of hunting pressure. When they become wary and flush farther out, some wingshooters change chokes. They may set up their barrels modified and modified.

One thing to consider, especially later in the hunting season, is larger shot sizes. This can be a helpful way to improve your pattern's effectiveness downrange.

Larger pellets tend to stay together longer. This allows the shot string to hold its shape and improve downrange accuracy. Many late-season hunters use more open chokes, but rely on larger pellets to reach out on those long birds. Larger pellets can do more damage, however, because they have more mass and energy. The pheasant hunter is most often better off with No. 6s or even No. 5s in the late season. The grouse hunter may start the season with No. 9s but drop down to No. 7½s by the end of the season.

Shot size is a way to slightly adjust the effectiveness of the pattern if the gun has fixed chokes (as on many older field guns). By adjusting the shot size, it's possible to improve the shot pattern's downrange effectiveness.

The seasoned wingshooter learns to adjust as the season wears on. Often, just a small change, like pellet size, can result in more downed birds and happier gun dogs.

Choosing the correct choke and loads for upland hunting can be important.

PART IX

General Advice

66

When buying a hunting dog, pay attention to breeding

GOING AFIELD WITH YOUR OWN DOG CAN BE ONE OF THE most satisfying aspects of bird hunting. When planning to buy a hunting dog, it is important to consider its bloodline and breeding. One of the most common upland hunting dogs is the Labrador retriever, a proven versatile breed that can retrieve waterfowl or flush upland game. It's a wonderful choice for the wingshooter. However, because the Labrador retriever is the most common family dog in America, there are breeders everywhere. Some specialize in selling cute puppies, some breed show dogs, and others actually breed hunting dogs. You need to fully research the breeder's background and the dog's bloodline to understand what kind of dog you are buying.

When you decide to buy a hunting dog, you must understand that you are getting an athlete. This is a dog that can handle the rigors of hunting long days in the field. Its hips, joints, and heart are hopefully bred to last. A hunting dog needs some smarts and a good temperament, but that's not really a prerequisite. A quality bloodline provides some assurance that the dog will be well suited for the field. Nothing is a guarantee, but if you research the breeder and the dog's bloodline, it should give you some idea of the type of dog you are buying.

Also, unless you are a seasoned dog trainer, it's probably best to avoid selecting the Alpha dog out of a litter. These dogs are higher maintenance and, as a rule, are a little more difficult to train. Some hunters prefer a hard-charging dog, but an Alpha dog can be hard-headed. These are best trained by someone who has a lot of field experience.

Hunting with your own dog is one of the most exciting and enjoyable aspects of going afield. For the wingshooter, few things are better than witnessing your dog perform well in the field. The bond created with your dog while hunting is special, and the memories can last a lifetime.

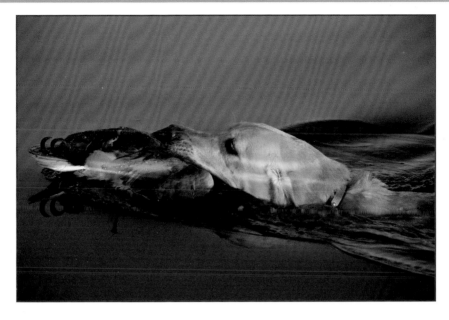

When selecting a hunting dog, be particular about breeding.

67

Flushing dogs vs. pointing dogs

A WELL-TRAINED HUNTING DOG CAN BE INDISPENSABLE IN the field. Also, wingshooting is more fun and entertaining when dogs are involved. The more you hunt with dogs, the more you can see their individual personalities and hunting instincts revealed.

For bird hunting, there are a few basic types of dogs: pointing dogs, flushing dogs, and retrievers. Retrievers and flushing dogs fall into the same category. Some breeds specialize more on retrieving and others tend to specialize in flushing. For example, the Labrador retriever, due to its larger size, tends to be considered more of a waterfowl-retrieving breed. Labs also make perfectly suitable flushing dogs, especially on birds such as pheasants and grouse. The smaller cocker spaniel and springer spaniel are considered flushing breeds. Both can retrieve waterfowl quite well. It all depends on what you need your dog to do based on the type of hunting you plan to do most.

The pointing dog specializes in finding and pointing upland birds. These dogs use their noses and legs to find game birds on the ground. They lock up on point when they locate their quarry. Pointing dogs can be a real pleasure to hunt with. They tend to run fast and cover lots of ground but then hold a steady point once the bird is located.

A well-trained and steady pointing dog is a wonderful hunting companion. There are many breeds to choose from: The quail hunter may prefer the English pointer, the New England bird hunter may favor a close-working Brittany, and the Western wingshooter may choose a wide-ranging German shorthair or English setter.

With the proper training, any of these breeds can hunt any upland bird. I've seen setters make some fine retrieves on ducks. It's certainly harder to keep these pointing breeds steady in a blind or boat while duck hunting, but it does happen.

Whether you choose a flushing dog or a pointing dog is really a matter of how you want to enjoy your time afield. If you are going to primarily chase waterfowl and hunt upland birds only a few times year, the Labrador retriever might be your best bet. If you are a serious quail hunter, a pointing dog is your best option. Selecting the right breed and type of dog can really add to your wingshooting experience.

Choosing a flushing dog or a pointing dog is really a matter of how you want to enjoy your time afield.

Practice restraint with an electric collar

TRAINING YOUR DOG IN THE OFF-SEASON IS A GREAT WAY to stay connected to bird hunting year-round. Many wingshooters ramp up the training in late summer as the hunting season grows near. Many dog trainers and bird hunters use an electric collar while training and hunting with their dogs. This type of collar is a training device that allows you to mildly shock a dog with the press of a button. The modern e-collar has many functions. Some have a pager function, and some even have GPS built in.

The e-collar is not without controversy among professional dog trainers. There is potential for misuse, but only in the wrong hands. The proper use of an e-collar allows a trainer to give a correction at a long distance, which can be very useful. A properly timed correction is much better than a correction delivered too late. Often, training is set back with a delayed correction. The e-collar can allow the trainer to be on time with a correction, which can lead to fewer corrections and stress on the dog in the long run.

One shortcoming of an e-collar is that it does not teach your dog anything. You can't control a dog with an electric shock. The inexperienced dog trainer can be led to believe that he can cure mistakes by enthusiastically pressing the button of an e-collar. Nothing could be farther from the truth. If the dog doesn't comprehend what the task is, a shock from the collar may only confuse it more.

The e-collar should only be used when a dog strays from the assigned task. It can be a useful and effective training tool, but only in the right hands.

An electric collar can be a useful and effective training tool but only in the right hands.

Think fly fishing when selecting a hunting vest

THE FLYFISHERMAN HAS TO CARRY EVERYTHING IN HIS vest that he will need while on the river. When fly fishing, the angler is actually wearing his tackle box. The bird hunter's needs are similar.

When you head into the field, you need to carry some essential items. Your vest should able to carry these items without weighing you down. I prefer a vest that distributes the weight of my gear across my shoulders. A well-designed vest does not shift or pull on the back of your neck, even with a bunch of shells and a few dead birds in it.

I also prefer a vest that includes some blaze orange on the back and shoulders. This is just a little added color for safety and is often legally required in some states.

Some hunters don't like having blaze orange on their vests, believing that birds can see them moving in on a point. I don't buy this at all. The birds will hear the dog and hunters—even feel the vibrations of their footsteps—well before they can see them. Having some orange on just makes good sense from a safety standpoint.

When selecting and trying on a new hunting vest, wear the same clothes you would wear in the field. Often, a shooter will wear a shirt and a sweater under his vest, so it needs to fit comfortably over several layers. When in doubt, go a size larger.

A properly fitting shooting vest should allow you to swing and mount the gun without the slightest restriction. Also, be careful if the vest has leather shoulder patches. This can be a sticky problem—literally—especially if you have a leather-covered butt pad, which may hang up on the shoulder patch.

Some shooters tend to use lighter vests during the early season. These can be much cooler to wear, especially on warm days or when covering a lot of territory. Some companies offer lightweight strap vests, which can be very cool and lightweight in the early season. Also, the straps are often adjustable, so it can be worn over a sweater or jacket in the late season.

The hunting vest is an important tool for the upland hunter.

Lastly, make sure your vest has all the features you need. A bird pouch in the back can be invaluable when hunting a long way from the truck. This allows you to stow your birds in your vest and continue to hunt. Pockets are also important. You can't have too many pockets!

The best shooting vest will have all the features you need without restricting your ability to mount the gun.

70

Selecting the perfect upland hunting boots

IT'S NOT EASY TO DEFINE THE PERFECT UPLAND HUNTING boot. Hunting conditions throughout the season can vary from very dry to very wet; there is no single boot that is perfect for all the conditions the bird hunter may face throughout the season. In the late season, you may need a boot with some insulation, whereas in the early season, you may prefer something lighter and more comfortable as you amble through your favorite bird covert.

I use three basic criteria when selecting a hunting boot: tread, weight, and waterproof material.

Let's begin at the bottom.

The proper upland boot must have a sole with quality tread for firm traction. I remember ordering a name-brand hunting boot thinking it was a great choice. It was a little muddy in the woods following a few days of rain on the first day I wore this boot, and it turned out that it had the worst tread for slippery, muddy hills. I was sliding around all afternoon and even fell once. The fact is that it could have been dangerous. I was hunting by myself, and luckily, nothing was injured except my pride. Be sure your boot has the proper tread for the conditions where you will be bird hunting.

Next, be sure your hunting boots are not too heavy. It is said that the average grouse hunter walks three miles per bird. That's a lot of heavy lifting! A heavy boot can be a drag to walk in all afternoon. Heavier boots tend to be uncomfortable and bulky, and a tired hunter is no match for a fast-flying upland target.

An upland boot should be waterproof. The uplands can be riddled with bogs, streams, and all kinds of wet conditions. Gore-Tex and other waterproof materials have done a lot to improve footwear for hunters. Boots made of these materials are lightweight and effective at keeping your feet dry and warm. Nothing feels worse than hiking for miles with wet feet as the temperature starts dropping.

Upland boots are made from a variety of materials: traditional leather, Cordura, rubber, and even kangaroo leather. These materials all work well in an upland boot. Leather-Cordura combinations are popular now. These boots are lightweight and durable.

My favorite material is kangaroo leather. Waterproof kangaroo boots are simply terrific for upland hunting. Kangaroo hide is extremely light-weight and comfortable. The very first time I put on a pair of these, I was a believer. Kangaroo hide is extremely durable and will hold up to brush, briars, thorns, and practically anything else. When my first pair wore out, I ordered another pair of Gore-Tex-lined kangaroo hunting boots the very next season.

When selecting an upland hunting boot, pay attention to details like tread, weight, materials, and waterproof material. (Photo courtesy of The Orvis Company)

It's important to break in your new hunting boots before heading into the field. Some boots require a longer break-in period than others: Leather boots need more break-in time than some man-made materials. However, my latest pair of kangaroo boots needed almost no breaking in.

To make your boots last longer, invest in a small boot dryer. These are cheap and efficient and can dry out wet boots in no time. Some boots are waterproof but not breathable. As your foot heats up, moisture builds up in the boot. A boot dryer will help keep your boots in good shape for the next day and for years to come.

Think, tread, weight, and waterproof material when purchasing your next pair of upland hunting boots.

Blaze orange for the upland hunter

ALWAYS WEAR BLAZE ORANGE WHEN TAKING TO THE FIELD for a hunt. Most states require hunters to wear a blaze orange hat and vest while hunting, especially during deer season. Some states also require wearing an orange hat during small-game seasons. Always check state regulations before heading into the woods. The safest thing to do is to always wear an orange hat and vest while upland hunting. The birds won't care, and it just might save your life!

Some vests are made with blaze orange material on the top half. You can also find hunting shirts that have orange material on the sleeves.

The upland hat, in my opinion, should always be orange. When hunting with a partner in thick cover, it can be difficult to see another person standing just a few yards away.

The grouse cover in New England can be extremely thick, especially in the early season. For this reason, my hunting buddies and I always wear blaze orange hats, but especially when hunting in tall grass or thick, dense cover.

Check your state hunting regulations for details on blaze orange requirements.

Blaze orange is a must for the upland hunter, especially in tall brush and when hunting with others.

Practice mounting your shotgun at home

THERE ARE TIMES WHEN LIFE GETS IN THE WAY AND YOU can't find the time you'd like for your sporting interests. Work, family, and other obligations simply don't allow you the time to go to the range and practice your shooting. When this is the case, try a little in-home practice to keep your shooting skills sharp.

Practice mounting the gun at home when you can't get to the shooting range.

One of the most important aspects of consistent accuracy is a steady head and a smooth gun mount. This is something you can practice at home without having to bust targets. New shooters can also greatly improve their skills by dry-mounting the gun at home. This can give you some reps without the effects of recoil.

There are a couple of points to remember when practicing your mount at home. One is to make sure you focus on something other than the bead when mounting. Pick a spot on the wall and pretend it's a flushing pheasant going straight away. Many times, a shooter will focus on the bead when mounting the gun. This can lead to a very bad habit. You want to avoid training your eye to lock in on the end of the gun. In essence, you are training yourself to aim instead of focusing on the bird. Certainly, you should peer down the rib every now and then to see if the eye and barrels are lining up correctly, but as a rule, keep your focus on that spot on the wall.

Also, keep your head still and raise the gun up to the shoulder and cheek. Often, a shooter will place the butt of the gun into the shoulder pocket first and then finish the gun mount by dropping the head down onto the stock. Dropping the head makes it very difficult to maintain a sharp focus on the bird. Practice mounting the gun smoothly, even in slow motion, until the mount feels natural to you. Develop the habit of pressing the gun into the cheek. The butt of the gun should slide smoothly into the shoulder pocket.

Also, be sure to practice swinging the gun as you bring the stock up to the shoulder and cheek. Most of the time, while shooting at moving targets, there is some swinging motion involved. This is excellent practice for learning how to swing and mount the gun in one smooth motion.

If you haven't been to the shooting range in a while, spend some time at home mounting the gun. You may be surprised at how much better you will shoot the next time you pull the trigger on moving targets.

Learn how to properly clean your shotgun

A WELL-DESIGNED SHOTGUN IS A reliable tool. You can run hundreds of rounds though it, and it will perform flawlessly. However, it's a good idea to perform some general maintenance on your gun to make sure it remains in good operating condition.

Wipe the entire gun down with a lightly oiled rag after every shooting or hunting session. This will remove moisture, sand, dust, and other debris from outside surfaces. Any untreated moisture can lead to rust and eventually pitting of the metal. Some oils are made for metal parts and others are made for the wood stock and forend. It is worth the extra effort to keep your shotgun clean and looking new.

Next is a thorough cleaning of the barrels and action. The barrels can have a good bit of powder residue built up in them after a few rounds of skeet or sporting clays. Use a good solvent made for cleaning the barrels. Also, use a toothbrush to give the action a scrubbing using a touch of the same solvent. This will help remove any built-up gunk or residue.

Cleaning a double-barrel shotgun can be quite easy. There are fewer parts to clean, and such guns are easy to break down and reassemble. An automatic shotgun can be a bit trickier to clean, so keep the gun's owner's manual handy as a guide to proper cleaning.

Finish cleaning your gun by lightly lubricating the action where there is metal-to-metal contact. When these parts are allowed to dry out, they can create function problems. A properly lubricated action and barrels will extend the life of your shotgun.

Finally, avoid storing your gun anywhere that gets too cold or too humid. This can cause condensation, which leads to rust. You can buy moisture absorbing systems from most hunting supply catalogs, a good idea when storing guns for long periods of time.

Find the right balance and weight for your shotgun

HAVE YOU EVER PICKED UP YOUR SHOOTING BUDDY'S shotgun and given it a few dry mounts? After downing a few imaginary birds with it, you find yourself saying, "I like the feel of this baby!" Most likely, you did like the balance and weight of the gun. Finding the proper balance point and weight in a shotgun can result in more effective shooting at the range.

Most often, the balance point of a double-barreled shotgun is at or near the hinge pin, and the best game guns often have a balance point that is at or near center. The purpose of establishing a balance point at the hinge pin is that it spreads the weight of the gun evenly between the hands. The clay shooter might decide to move the balance point so that the gun feels a bit barrel-heavy, the theory being that extra weight in the barrels makes it easier to swing and follow through on passing clay targets.

The bird hunter might want a balance point on the hinge pin or slightly behind it. This can create the sensation of a light-barreled gun that's quicker to point and shoot.

Most guns are built with a specific balance point, which is most often directly over the hinge pin. To change this, you can reduce the weight of the stock by hollowing out some wood. Or, you can add some weight to the forend with lead tape. Each of these can change the balance characteristics of the gun. See your gunsmith if you want to alter the balance point of your shotgun.

The weight of a gun should really depend on its intended use. Field guns tend to be lighter for ease of carry on long hikes through the countryside. The average upland gun weighs somewhere between 5½ and 6½ pounds. Obviously, the smaller gauges will be lighter, which is why upland hunters often choose a twenty- or twenty-eight-gauge over a twelve-gauge.

The clay shooter often favors a heavier gun for several reasons. A heavier gun tends to swing and follow through with less effort (the duck hunter may want a slightly heavier gun for the same reasons). Also, a heavier gun, when matched with lighter target loads, can help reduce felt recoil. Target loads in a heavy twelve-gauge gun can really be pleasant to shoot, even during 100 rounds of sporting clays.

The perfect combination of balance and weight is mostly a matter of personal preference. Finding the right feel in a shotgun can make it easier to point and shoot, leading to more success at the range.

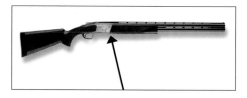

Most often, the balance point of a gun is at, or very near, the hinge pin. (Photo courtesy of Browning)

75

Check current regulations before hunting

IT WAS A WARM AND SUNNY AUTUMN AFTERNOON. WE intended to hit one of our favorite grouse coverts near the small town of Ira, Vermont. My hunting partner released his female setter out of her crate. She shot out of it like a cannon ball, eager to find us some birds. We jumped an old stonewall and started walking across a hillside. A few minutes into our hunt, the dog winded something and then locked up on point. We flanked the dog on either side and readied our guns for a flush. As we walked past the dog on point, a bird flushed up into thinly covered canopy. My hunting buddy pulled his trigger, and I could see a bird fall back down through the trees.

When the dog went to find the bird, she was in no mood to bring it out of some thicker brush. My hunting partner bushwhacked his way to the downed bird and pulled out a woodcock. My first reaction was confusion. I thought he was shooting at a grouse, and I wasn't completely certain that woodcock season had opened. Sheepishly, I asked my hunting partner if woodcock season was open yet. He looked at me a little puzzled. Then, he shook his head and said, "I thought it opened this past Wednesday?" We had one of those awkward moments of silence, and then we started laughing. He was right. Woodcock season had been open for almost a week. I just lost my head for a minute there. I apologized to my buddy for the confusion, and we moved on to hunt more of the covert.

This can happen more often than you think, and shooting game out of season can carry some hefty fines and even the loss of hunting privileges if you're not careful. I happen to duck hunt in several different states with many different hunting zones, so it can be difficult to keep up with when the seasons open and close in each state and zone. Also, you need to know where the boundary lines are drawn. The same river or lake can be split into different hunting zones.

Also, be aware of bag limits. For upland game, it can be fairly cut-and-dry. When hunting waterfowl, it can be a little more confusing. For example, in Vermont it reads, "the daily limit of 6 ducks may include no harlequin ducks and no more than 4 mallards (2 of which may be hens), 1 black duck, 3 wood ducks, 2 pintails, 1 canvasback, 2 redheads, 4 scaup, and 4 scoters." As you can see, you need to be careful when you are closing in on your limit.

Be sure to always check the hunting regulations in the states that you hunt. This is an important part of being a safe and ethical wingshooter.

General Tips for the Upland Hunter

76

Understanding upland bird habitat

HABITAT IS SIMPLY WHERE UPLAND BIRDS CHOOSE TO LIVE, feed, breed, and roost. The upland hunter's job is to find the most likely spots or areas that hold birds. Some coverts are small whereas others, particularly out West, seem to roll on for as far as the eye can see.

The best bird coverts are typically a combination of natural features that include water, food, and protection from predators. When you find an area that has an abundance of these features, you will have found a good place to hunt.

Each species of upland bird requires very different-looking cover, although multiple species may be found in overlapping cover. Bobwhite quail cover looks very different from that of the ruffed grouse. Some upland birds such as the ring-necked pheasant have a very wide geographical range. This means that pheasant cover in Iowa can look vastly different from pheasant habitat in Montana. The look of a covert can vary due to geography and the desired habitat of each species. Study the game birds you are going after in the habitat they prefer. It doesn't take long to identify and recognize good bird habitat in any given area.

One common denominator in upland bird cover is protection from predators. Creek bottoms surrounded by small trees often produce pheasants in the Western states. Clumps of brush in an otherwise open grass prairie tend to hold sharp-tailed grouse. Clusters of thickets sometimes produce coveys of quail.

Upland birds are not often found in the open, and there is a reason for this. It's called survival. Overhead predators such as hawks can easily pick off game birds that linger in the open. Some of the most productive ruffed grouse covert features evergreen trees along its edges. Food and water are important factors in upland bird habitat, but don't overlook protection from predation.

Productive bird cover can be very diverse. Many factors such as geography, type of available game birds, food sources, and protective cover can come into play.

77

Keep it light when quail hunting

SOME STUDENTS COME TO AN ORVIS SHOOTING SCHOOL to prepare for the upcoming season or a hunting trip. Many are there because they have been invited to hunt quail with a friend or business associate. Fewer hunts are more special than a traditional southern bobwhite quail hunt.

Because hunting quail can be unique, there are a few details to consider. (For additional pointers for shooting quail, refer to tip No. 58.)

A quail is a small game bird, so you might want to consider selecting a smaller gauge gun. A twelve-gauge is really too much gun; a twenty-eight-gauge is considered ideal for shooting the smallest upland game birds because it has the same diameter shot pattern as the twelve-gauge but less pellet density. The smaller shell of the twenty-eight-gauge contains fewer pellets, but the pattern is not any smaller than that of a twelve-gauge with the same choke restriction.

Many shooters think that smaller gauges put them at a disadvantage, believing that they have smaller patterns. This simply is not true. In fact, the pattern of a twenty-eight-gauge is extremely effective because the twenty-eight-gauge has a fairly short shot string. This means that most of the pellets reach the bird at the same time.

The .410 is a fun gun to shoot, but its shot string is quite a bit longer. I've never been a real fan of it until recently. I always believed that the .410 would cripple a lot of birds. On a recent quail hunt, I noticed that our guide had a pretty little Browning .410 hanging off of the quail buggy. He noticed me eyeing it and suggested that I try it. When I put my hands on it, I noticed it was .410. "What the heck?" I thought.

On the first covey, I cleanly downed two birds. I began to warm up to the little gun after that. We hunted a few more hours, and the gun preformed beautifully. After that afternoon, I began to look at the .410 differently. One noticeable feature was that the gun had little to no recoil.

This model was built on a twenty-eight-gauge frame, which added weight, but that only helped it soak up what little recoil there was. The .410 is a great choice for close-range bird hunting, but it has its limitations. If you are hunting wild quail, you might want to consider a twenty- or twenty-eight-gauge. Wild birds create a bit more of challenge because they tend to flush farther out and fly a little more quickly.

Finally, use fairly open chokes and smaller pellet sizes. Improved cylinder is the most common choke for quail shooting. Occasionally, it helps to put a modified choke in the second barrel, especially if the birds aren't holding tight.

Most target loads for the twenty-eight-gauge are perfect for quail hunting. No. 8 shot with a ¾-ounce load patterns beautifully and is an ideal choice for quail hunting.

When hunting quail, sub-gauge guns and lighter loads can be very effective.

78

Hunting pants or chaps?

A DURABLE, QUALITY PAIR OF HUNTING PANTS OR CHAPS is indispensable to the upland hunter. The best upland habitat contains briars, brambles, saplings, vines, thorns, and other nasty stuff that the hunter must walk (or bull) his way through.

One season, a hunting buddy showed up on opening day with a new pair of brush pants. They looked a little lightweight for New England grouse and woodcock cover, but I didn't think much of it at the time. We started to follow the dog, and pretty soon, we came up on some nasty early-season cover. We pressed on, eager to keep up with the dog. Once we came out the other side of the thick brush, I noticed my buddy looking down at his new pants. At first glance, it looked as if he had "left the barn door open." However, upon closer inspection, it was clear that my friend's pants had been torn open. The thorny bushes had ripped a gaping hole in a very delicate spot. At the end of the hunt, his pants looked as if they had been run through a blender.

Obviously, these pants weren't made of the proper material for walking through thick cover. They were made of lightweight cotton, designed for walking through grass and light brush during warm weather. Hunting pants are made from a variety of materials. Often, the front is reinforced for added protection from clinging brush. The most common materials used are Cordura, Ventile, waxed cotton, Gore-Tex, Hawthorne Cloth, nylon, and cotton. Be sure you are choosing a hunting pant that can stand up to conditions you are likely to encounter. If you mostly walk the open grasslands of the West, you might not need as much briar protection. If you chase pheasants in thicker cover, you should look for a heavier, more protective pant.

Chaps are also a good alternative. They are designed to be worn over the pants and, depending on the material, can provide excellent briar protection. I like to hunt in chaps in the late season when the weather turns cold. They provide protection from the briars and add a layer of warmth.

The upland hunter should wear a quality pair of hunting pants or chaps, especially when the cover is think and thorny.

79

Use the off-season time for scouting

The off-season is the perfect time to scout for new coverts.

THE OFF-SEASON IS THE PERFECT TIME DO A LITTLE scouting for your favorite upland game. Summer is the perfect time to scour the uplands and get a little off-season work done. For many hunters, this is also a way to stay connected to the sport they love even when they can't legally hunt.

I look at scouting for birds two ways. First, it can be a way to see what's happening in the woods and to get a sense of how many birds there will be in the upcoming hunting season. I'm always curious to see how the winter may have affected the bird population. Also, in summer, it's fun to see how successful the mating season went. If conditions were favorable in spring, there should be more successful nesting attempts. Nothing beats putting boots on the ground if you want to find clutches of birds still bunched up in family units.

Another benefit of scouting is that it gives the hunter time to look for and locate new bird cover. There are many reasons why a hunter may lose a covert or two between seasons. It seems as if someone is always posting land that had been open for hunting. When this happens, don't be afraid to knock on doors and politely ask for permission to hunt when you see newly posted signs. Some landowners just want hunters to ask first. They may want to know who is hunting on their land and when they plan to be on the property.

Finding new and possibly productive places to hunt really gets you excited for the upcoming hunting season.

Scouting can also be an effective way to get your dog in shape for the upcoming season. Nothing beats putting a bird dog through its paces on wild bids. Be sure to check state regulations on this.

Most limit training seasons on wild birds to protect the young ones. It's not a good idea to disturb upland game birds during the spring nesting season.

80

GPS—next to a dog, it's a hunter's best friend

HAVE YOU EVER GOTTEN LOST? IF SO, YOU KNOW IT CAN BE a stressful experience. I will admit that I have gotten turned around in the woods on more than one occasion. The last time it happened, I walked right out of the woods and into the local sporting goods store. Since then, I never go hunting without my GPS.

A GPS (Global Positioning System) unit is a satellite-based navigation system that can track your location to within a few feet. This can be indispensable when you're not really sure where you parked your SUV.

You should always have an idea of the direction back to the trail or vehicle. This keeps your head in the game and helps confirm your readings when you check the GPS.

The GPS can be a valuable tool for the upland hunter. Most units have a color display and topographic maps built in. My latest unit even has the depths of nearby lakes and ponds. I have used this to run a river in the fog during duck season. These features allow the upland hunter to understand a covert even if he has never hunted it before. This also makes the GPS a wonderful tool when hunting in another state or territory. They can help establish the best entry and exit points along with determining spots you may want to avoid.

Also, you can store the locations of your favorite coverts in your device. You simply pull up your list of waypoints and plan your hunts for the day. A hunter can even return to a spot he hunted years ago. This can save scouting time and allow you more time to hunt.

It's still a good idea to carry a compass and always pay attention to the sun and other landmarks, but a GPS can be a bird hunter's best friend. Just don't let the dog know!

Every hunter should be prepared and carry a GPS on every hunt.

81

Learn to be an effective dogless hunter

MANY BIRD HUNTERS TAKE TO THE FIELD WITHOUT A DOG. Some can't afford a dog and others might be between dogs or have not yet decided which breed they prefer. A dog can help locate and flush game more effectively, but the hunter who knows his quarry and its habitat can find birds without a dog.

Hunting without a dog is more effective when two or more hunters are involved. A small group can cover more ground, which means there's a greater chance to walk up on and flush a bird. A solo hunter will often walk right past a hidden pheasant.

When hunting in a group, it's a good idea to have one hunter walk through the bird-looking areas of a cover. When he encounters cover that looks as if it might hold birds, one hunter should push through that thicker stuff, hopefully flushing the bird and giving one of his partners a shot. In essence, one hunter becomes the dog.

It's a good idea to rotate the brush-busting hunter from time to time, so that everyone gets a turn as the outside shooter.

It's important to be ready to shoot in spots where you expect a flush. An experienced dogless hunter recognizes areas that look promising. Also, if you've hunted the same cover a number of times, often the flushes occur in the same spots. This could be a fence line, brush pile, a particular apple tree, or blow-down. Often, birds will flush as they run out of protective cover at the end of a food plot. When approaching these areas, move in slowly, ready to shoot.

Finally, pause occasionally while moving through cover. This can make birds nervous. Many times, a bird will flush as soon as the hunter starts walking again. This can be a very productive way to produce flushes, especially for the solo hunter. Take your time when moving through bird-looking cover. Move slowly but steadily, and be sure to kick every bit of cover along the way. It doesn't take much to hide a game bird, and they will often let you walk right over them. Stop every so often to make reluctant birds fly.

Hunting with a dog adds to the fun, but you can effectively hunt upland birds without one.

The dogless hunter should stop frequently where the covert looks birdie. Also, when hunting with a buddy, take turns pushing through the thicker brush. These methods can sometimes produce a flush.

82

Beepers vs. bells

THE UPLAND HUNTER TYPICALLY USES A COLLAR OF SOME type on his hunting dog to help track its movements. This can be very helpful when the dog is on point, out of sight because of thick cover, or moving quickly into the distance.

There are two types of collars the dog handler can use: a belled collar or beeper-type collar. The belled collar jingles as the dog runs about in its effort to locate birds. Once it locates the birds and locks up on point, the bell stops ringing. This tells the hunter that the dog has winded some birds and is on point.

The bell is a traditional tool for hunting with a pointing dog. Some bird hunters believe that the ringing of the bells alerts or warns birds that hunters are in the area. Most believe this is nonsense, and that the bells work just fine. There is no real data to support this either way. Bird hunters just have hunches on this subject.

A beeper collar can be set up in a few different ways depending on how you want it to work. In its basic "run" mode, it may sound every five or ten seconds while the dog moves through cover. Once the dog goes on point, the beeper tone changes or the unit stops beeping.

One important feature of a beeper collar is its location function. The hunter presses a button on the remote, and the beeper responds with a distinct sound that reveals the dog's location. This can be very helpful when you can't see the dog or it's locked on point. This often happens when the grass is tall or the cover is very thick.

Some pointing dogs are trained to work out ahead of the hunters at longer distances. A locator function on your beeper collar can be helpful when hunting with such wide-ranging dogs. A dog may be on point far ahead of the hunters. A location beep can help the hunters find the dog and move into position for the shot.

Some hunters prefer to use the beeper collar manually. This works fine in areas of lighter cover or with close-working dogs. If you can see the dog work, you may only need to operate the collar on the manual setting.

When running two dogs, or when hunting in thick cover, a beeper collar makes it easier to locate a dog.

If you happen to lose the dog for a period of time, you can locate it by simply pressing a button. This application works fine on preservation hunts and released birds when dogs tend to work closer and the cover is not as thick.

The beeper collar can be useful when running two dogs. Doing so with two high-energy pointing dogs can be chaotic at times, and the beeper collar helps keep things straight when multiple dogs are running through the woods.

Multiple-dog collars feature different tones for each dog, and the location sound can be customized for each one. Some offer sounds like a hawk or other common bird, and others vary in tone duration.

Some hunters run their dogs with both the bell and beeper collar. This allows them to hear the ringing of the bell but also helps locate a dog that's on point somewhere out of sight.

Habitat conditions often determine which collar setup is best for the hunter and his dog.

Work into the wind when hunting a covert

WORK INTO THE WIND WHEN BIRD HUNTING. THIS CAN allow the dog to pick up the scent of birds concealed in a patch of cover.

A dog's nose is truly amazing. Close to 15 percent of a dog's brain is dedicated to interpreting odors, and approximately 50 percent of its nasal passages is devoted to collecting scent. Given the fact that most bird dogs have big noses, this is an impressive statistic. We humans cannot easily comprehend how much more advanced a dog's nose is than ours. A dog trainer I know put it this way: "Comparing a dog's sense of smell to a human's is like comparing our brain to a dog's." A dog's sense of smell is vastly superior to ours. We may beat them on intellect, but a dog's sense of smell is exponentially greater than ours.

Armed with his super nose, you can improve the dog's ability to locate birds by working into the wind. This can be especially important when scent conditions are poor. Dogs usually have a better time picking up the scent of a bird when there's a little dampness on the ground. An early morning mist coupled with a light breeze

Working into the wind can make it easier for your dog to scent the birds.

often provides perfect scenting conditions for the dog. Scent can be almost impossible for a dog to detect when conditions are very dry and the wind is light. For this reason, hunting is often most productive early or late in the day. At midday, the combination of sun, wind, and low humidity can cause even the best dog to run right over a covey of tight-sitting quail.

Essential items for your hunting vest

1. Ammunition
2. Cell phone
3. GPS
4. Compass
5. Multi-tool
6. Water
7. Extra batteries
8. Waterproof matches
9. Small flashlight
10. Extra socks

Make sure to carry some essential items every time you go afield.

THIS IS A LIST OF ITEMS THAT SHOULD PROVE USEFUL ON every trip. Some of them may not be needed on shorter hunts, but all of them may prove invaluable on any hunt. When planning an extended hunt, plan carefully and load your vest accordingly.

Most wingshooters carry extra shells, a phone, and a knife or multi-tool. Not many carry water bottles, maps, extra socks, or batteries, but one day they'll wish they had!

Don't mix extra batteries in with your shells. Most AA batteries are about the same size as a twenty-eight-gauge shell. It can be easy to slip one down the barrel if you're not careful. I keep my extra batteries in a ziplock bag in a separate pocket. This keeps them dry and prevents them for being mixed in with my shells.

It's also good idea to keep a gunning box in the vehicle. This should include a first-aid kit for yourself and for the dog.

Many hunting supply catalogs offer specialized first-aid kits for dogs. These include forceps, which are handy for removing thorns or porcupine quills and the like.

A prepared, well-stocked gunning box can make or break a day of hunting. I once brought twenty-gauge shells and a twenty-eight-gauge gun to a hunt. It was too far from home to go back, so I worked the dog while my hunting buddy did the shooting. After that, I made sure to keep my gunning box supplied with a variety of shells and to leave it in the back of the SUV throughout the season.

85

If you're new to dog training, go see a pro

TRAINING A DOG TO HUNT BIRDS CAN BE REWARDING and sometimes even more fun than the hunting itself. Helping your dog evolve into an effective field hunter can be a satisfying journey. Training is a year-round activity designed to keep you and your dog connected while developing and maintaining the skills necessary to find and flush game birds.

Training a dog to hunt upland game or to retrieve ducks is a simple process based on repetition. There are gradual goals your dog must achieve and build upon before he becomes a productive hunting companion. This is not a process that can be done overnight.

If you are new to dog training, I recommend that you read up on proven training methods and seek the help of a professional trainer. It helps to have someone with years of experience to lean on. Many trainers will work with owners and their dogs, offering clinics and problem-specific lessons designed to help you and your dog become more effective in the field. Keep in mind that it is not always the dog that needs the help. All bred-to-hunt dogs have the genetics and instincts to make them effective hunters; we just have to learn how to help them develop those skills.

Always keep training fun for you and your dog. It should not be stressful or exhausting. Watch your dog's body language. He will tell you when he is confused or stressed.

The best dog trainers are calm and patient, and they lead the dog with calm authority. Also, remember to keep training sessions short. It's always better to end with your dog wanting more than to overtrain and wear him out. Spend ten to fifteen minutes each day, maybe twice each day if you have time. Most dogs light up when they know they are going out for a training session. It's what they love to do, and they will let you know it.

A professional dog trainer will help you mold your hunting partner and help you avoid the common pitfalls of dog training as you and your dog progress into a well-oiled hunting team.

A professional trainer can help you and your dog progress in the field.

Ten Tips for the Waterfowl Hunter

86

Finding waterfowl—be where they want to go

ONE OF THE MOST IMPORTANT SKILLS IN SUCCESSFUL duck hunting is determining where the ducks want to go. This would seem like common sense, and it is, but knowing where the ducks are and predicting where they want to land can be challenging. I've often set up in areas that looked like perfect duck habitats, but for whatever reason, the birds chose to land on the other side of the marsh. This can be due to food availability, wind direction, or other factors. The waterfowler invests a great deal of time and effort in setting up his decoys and concealing his blind, but none of that does any good if the ducks don't want to land where he has set up. Where you choose to set up can be more important than how you set up.

Scouting can be a waterfowl hunter's most productive tool. You could have ten honey holes to pick from on opening morning, but the ducks may only want to be in one or two of those spots. Scouting allows you to narrow the options. Keep in mind that these can change from week to week or even day to day.

Finding the right location can make all the difference when hunting waterfowl. For example, sometimes ducks will want to land on just one side of the river. At other times, they will favor the far end of a corn field. Some advanced scouting can give you an idea of where they like to settle.

Lastly, don't be afraid to pick up and move if the ducks are not lighting in your area. A quick change of location can put you in the right spot for some great shooting.

87

Use the proper amount of duck decoys in your setup

THE NUMBER OF DECOYS IN YOUR HUNTING SPREAD HAS much to do with getting ducks to cooperate. Many waterfowl hunters subscribe to the "more is better" theory, meaning that the more decoys you have out there, the better your chances of pulling in ducks. Larger decoy spreads do seem to attract more birds, especially when hunting in large fields or vast expanses of open water and can also help when you are hunting where there are incentives for the ducks to land elsewhere, such as in a nearby refuge.

A large spread may include hundreds, even thousands, of decoys depending on the situation. Goose hunters often use trailer loads of decoys of various numbers. A smaller spread will be just as effective on smaller ponds, sloughs, and potholes.

When using a smaller setup, make sure you have proper spacing between your decoys. This gives the appearance that the ducks are content and maximizes the effectiveness of the decoys you deploy. Decoys that are tightly packed appear nervous or unrealistic to passing flocks.

Finally, don't be afraid to mix it up a little. Throwing a pintail decoy with its brighter color scheme into a spread of mallard decoys often can attract other species. Also, mixing in different species of ducks or adding some goose blocks can make your spread seem more realistic.

If you have the time and resources, setting out more decoys can be effective. When you have to go small, maximize the efficiency of your spread, so that passing ducks will be interested.

Setting out more decoys will often attract more ducks. When you have to go lighter, maximize the efficiency of your small spread so that ducks will be interested.

88

Rig 'em right and add some movement to your decoy spread

THE MORE NATURAL YOUR DECOYS LOOK, THE BETTER the chances are of attracting ducks. Find ways to make them appear as realistic as possible. There are a number of options the hunter has that will make those decoys look alive.

One handy tip is to rig some of your decoys with their weights off of the tail of the keel. This ensures that they will be facing different directions, which is how most puddle ducks look when they are content. When all the decoys are pointed in the same direction, this gives the impression that the birds are nervous and are about to take flight. I typically rig about a quarter of my decoys from the tail end of the keel to give my spread a more natural appearance.

Also, introduce some variety to your decoy setup. Add a few full-body decoys along the shoreline or place them in shallow water. Mix in different body types, too. A few feeding and resting decoys will add to the realism of your spread. On larger decoy spreads, mix in a few family groups.

Finally, put some motion into your decoy spread. It can be tough to get ducks to land in a spread if the floating decoys are completely still. This is very unnatural-looking.

Ducks with motorized wings are popular (where legal, of course). Motion decoys can be very effective at pulling ducks in when they are used correctly. These can really make your setup more visible to ducks in the air. However, some hunters don't like to use them, especially later in the season. The thought here is that the ducks become decoy-shy and dislike the motorized wing action.

I like to add floating full-body decoys when the breeze is up a little. The wind blows them around slightly and adds motion to the spread.

A weight with a cord that attaches to one of more decoys called a "jerk string" can be the perfect way to add motion when needed. The hunter pulls the cord to add motion to the decoys, giving the appearance of ducks feeding on the water. This can be very effective on days when there is little or no wind.

You can also try "quivering" duck decoys. I use one that looks like a duck feeding with its head in the water. I like to put this near the landing zone because the ducks will often fly right in toward it. Rig your decoys correctly and add some motion to improve the effectiveness of your spread.

Which is real and which is a motion decoy? Creating some movement in your decoy spread can make it look more realistic.

89

Create a landing zone for incoming ducks

ONE OF THE MOST IMPORTANT ELEMENTS TO CONSIDER when setting out decoys is to establish a natural landing zone for the ducks. How and where you place your decoys can greatly affect how and where the ducks will settle into your decoys. The best and most simple rule to follow is this: Place your decoys where you *don't* want the ducks to land. This means setting up your spread so that you leave a hole in your pattern where you want the birds to land, obviously in range of your shotgun. Your decoys should prevent the ducks from landing in the areas that are out of range.

Also, your setup should help lead incoming ducks into your pre-determined landing zone.

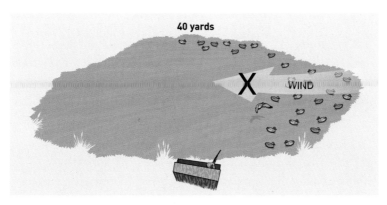

Create a landing zone for the ducks in your decoy spread.

One popular decoy pattern is what's known as the J or J-Hook pattern. Set some decoys in a line downwind of the blind to help lead the ducks toward the landing zone. Use other decoys as the hook in the J. This will deter the incoming ducks from flying too far past your setup and encourage them to land in front of the blind.

Don't be afraid to adjust your decoys occasionally, especially if the wind direction changes or the ducks are not coming in the way you planned. Simple adjustments can create a more effective landing zone.

Create an effective landing zone when you place your decoys. This will help bring passing ducks into shooting range and result in a more successful hunt.

90

Pay attention to wind direction

WIND DIRECTION IS IMPORTANT BECAUSE DUCKS WILL settle into your decoys from the downwind side. Ducks invariably approach and land into the wind. This makes sense if you think about it; the birds can glide in on a headwind and drop down to the water more efficiently. A headwind allows ducks to control their approach and to manage their landing with less danger.

The duck hunter should set up his decoys (and blind if possible) according to the direction of the wind. Place some decoys downwind with some blocker decoys just above the blind. A flock of ducks will often circle the decoys a number of times to get themselves correctly downwind for their final approach. On the last pass, the ducks will ride the headwind right into your pre-determined landing zone. If the wind direction changes, be prepared to adjust the decoys. You may have to rearrange them several times over the course of the day.

Ducks almost always approach the decoys from the easiest angle. If you are hunting on a pond surrounded by tall trees, they will most likely arrive and depart over the lowest bunch of trees. This depends on wind direction, of course.

When setting up for a hunt, pay attention to your surroundings, and take note of the easiest way for the ducks to approach. This can be very important if you are hunting in flooded timber or on a beaver pond of flowage that is surrounded by trees. If the wind is blowing out to an opening in the trees, you can almost guarantee that the ducks will approach from that angle.

Reading the wind is a big help in understanding how the ducks will approach the decoys. The seasoned duck hunter checks the wind first and then arranges his decoy spread accordingly.

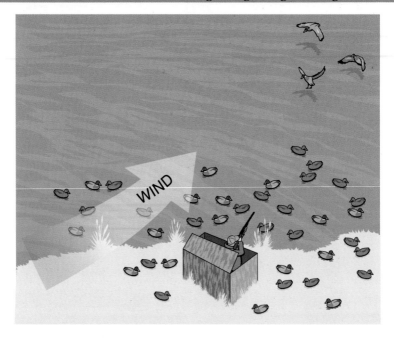

Wind direction will often dictate how the ducks will settle into your decoys. They will almost always want to approach and land into the wind.

91

Cover up for waterfowl

A LOT OF EFFORT GOES INTO SETTING UP CORRECTLY FOR a duck hunt. It starts with running the boat up the river or across the marsh. Time is spent setting up the blind and perhaps dozens of decoys. Often, the littlest detail can make or break a hunt.

One morning, my hunting partner and I had a flock of ducks working our decoy spread. I worked the call carefully to keep them interested. They circled around our setup twice, cupped their wings, and were getting ready to make their final approach to our landing zone. It was looking like a prefect start to our morning. My hunting buddy said, "Get ready, they're coming in."

Suddenly, they broke off and scrambled into the air. I couldn't believe it! They had looked committed, but there was something about our setup that they didn't like. Puzzled, I looked over to my partner, and then it hit me. He wasn't wearing a facemask.

"Did you bring a facemask?" I asked. He looked at me, shocked. "Damn," he said, "I forgot to put in on." About ten minutes later, another flock of ducks showed up. This time, my buddy's face was covered up with a camo mask. The ducks circled our decoys and then came right in. Our hunt was a success, and things only improved during the rest of the morning.

From an incoming duck's perspective, a hunter's face can stick out like a sore thumb. If you could look at overhead photographs of hunters in a blind looking up without masks on, you would see why it's important to wear cover-up. A hunter's face sticks out like a bright light in a sea of camouflage. Wary ducks, especially later in the season, can spot hunters' faces a long way off. All species of ducks have highly-developed vision on which they rely for flying and survival. They can see colors and details that the human eye would have trouble picking up.

It's natural to want to watch ducks as they are coming in. The hunter working the call needs to see the ducks in order to read their movements. Covering up the face can allow you to carefully peek at the birds as they fly overhead. However, be careful to keep movements to a minimum.

Ducks can also be spooked by hunters moving around in the blind, shifting their shotguns, or digging for extra shells.

Cover your hands as well. A sudden glare or movement can prevent ducks from coming in.

If possible, set up so that the sun is at your back. This can keep you in the shadows and prevent the sun from creating glare off of yourself or your blind. Also, incoming ducks will be landing into the sun. This can make it harder for them to spot danger as they approach. Also, whenever possible, use natural shadow and shade to help conceal your presence. Little details like this can make a difference.

Be sure to cover your face when duck hunting. Ducks have keen vision and pick up subtle details as they fly overhead.

92

Call softly and carry a big gun

I LOVE BLOWING A DUCK CALL! FEW MOMENTS IN HUNTING are more satisfying than having a distant flock of ducks respond to your call.

I must admit that I have scared away as many ducks with my calling as I have called in. Convincing a duck to turn and commit to my decoys is half the fun of hunting waterfowl. Sometimes, the ducks don't cooperate, but other times they do.

There is a lot that goes into properly operating a duck call, and there are many calls to learn and perfect. Perhaps knowing when *not* to call can be the most important lesson. Most veteran duck callers will tell you that the closer the ducks get, the quieter you should be. This is sound advice. Louder calling is for getting the ducks' attention. As they fly progressively closer, the volume and tone should become softer. Calling too aggressively as the ducks commit will likely push them away.

Learn to read the ducks and how they respond to your calling. Some days, you might only have to offer soft, little quacks and a light feeding chuckle. At other times, the birds might prefer a louder, more aggressive calling style. As a rule, it's necessary to call more loudly during windy conditions and more softly on calm mornings. It's all up to the ducks. Most often softer calling, or no calling, as the ducks approach is the best policy.

I've had ducks come in without blowing a peep. They just liked the look of the decoys, and in they came. The goal is to convince passing ducks that your decoys are real and content in their location. Adjust your calling style and volume by watching the ducks in the air. Stop calling when they begin their approach and have put their feet down to land in you decoy spread. Stop calling and start shooting!

Calling a duck can be very exciting, but you need to learn how to read the ducks in the air and adjust your calling style accordingly. As a rule, the closer they get, the softer and less you call.

93

The correct sight picture for pass-shooting ducks

MANY DUCK HUNTERS COME TO AN ORVIS SHOOTING School and want help on how to improve their success when shooting passing ducks. This can be a difficult and challenging situation.

When shooting passing ducks, it's best to use the speed and line of the bird to help develop the correct lead. One of the easiest ways to do this is to picture your lead instinctively. The most common mistake on a crossing bird is that the gun is mounted too soon. If the gun is mounted to the shoulder and cheek too early, there is a greater temptation for the eyes to focus on the barrels and not the bird. Once the eyes lock in on the barrels, the swing and follow-through are lost. It is difficult to develop the proper lead when the eyes are seeing the barrels rather than the bird.

Most shooters use a swing-through technique when pass-shooting ducks. Swing-through is an excellent way to develop the proper lead, but the wingshooter should be mindful of when to mount the gun. To develop the correct lead instinctively, swing along the flight path of the bird. As your eyes and gun barrel draw out ahead of the bird, mount the gun and take the shot. This allows you to picture the lead without the gun being in the mounted position too long. This also allows for a smoother follow-through. If the eyes are focused on the bird and not on the barrels, the gun tends to effortlessly swing ahead of the target.

The most common mistake in pass-shooting is that the shooter quickly mounts the gun to the shoulder when the bird is in sight, waits for the bird to gain ground, and then frantically tries to swing ahead of the target. Swinging ahead of the bird and mounting the gun should become one seamless motion. This allows for better focus on the target and less temptation to aim with the muzzle.

With practice, the speed and pace of the bird helps the shooter to develop the proper sight picture.

So much about shooting instinctively is misunderstood. Many shotgun shooters think that instinctive shooting means you always shoot at the bird, and that you don't really need to lead the target. This is simply not true. The instinctive shooter does see lead, it's just that his focus is much more on the bird and less on the gun. The instinctive shooter is aware that his muzzle is ahead of the target, but does not use the barrel to measure or maintain the lead. The instinctive shooter pictures lead but does not measure it.

To shoot instinctively, you trust that the eyes and hands are capable of swinging ahead and on line with the bird. Often the best shots are the ones during which you trust the sight picture with the eyes and just shoot. The most awkward shots are the ones during which the shooter hesitates, measuring to see if his lead is correct. That split second lost while checking to see if things are right invariably leads to a miss behind the target.

The shooter's hand–eye coordination is best when he simply gets it out of his own way and trust it. For best results, instinctively swing through the bird and picture the lead without second-guessing your ability. The results may surprise you.

Pass-shooting ducks can be challenging. (Photo courtesy of Jay Cassell)

94

Select the right duck gun

SELECTING THE PROPER SHOTGUN FOR WATERFOWL hunting can be a simple task once you understand what you need it to do.

First, let's begin with gauge. The vast majority of waterfowl hunters choose the twelve-gauge. Ducks are big, strong game birds. A twelve-gauge shotgun delivers enough pellets to take them down effectively. Unless you are shooting decoying ducks, the smaller gauges do not pack enough punch.

Also, when hunting ducks, it's best to use larger pellet sizes such as No. 2s, 3s, and 4s. The larger capacity of a twelve-gauge shell can carry more of these larger pellets to the target. This creates a denser shot pattern for cleaner kills. When used on longer, more difficult shots, the sub gauges can produce more wounded or crippled birds. No waterfowl hunter wants to cripple birds. An ethical hunter wants them killed and downed cleanly every time.

Also, most duck hunters tend to favor semiautomatic or pump-action shotguns because duck hunting can be hard on a pretty upland shotgun. There is often rain and mud to contend with, duck blinds, unruly retrievers, and water-filled boats. The waterfowl gun endures a lot of abuse under harsh conditions.

The semi-auto shotgun is perfectly suited for the waterfowl hunter. It is often stowed under the decoys during a long and rocky boat ride, or it is stuffed into a cart that is dragged through a muddy cornfield in the dark. The duck gun has to be able to handle abuse!

The duck blind can sometimes be a cold and wet place. It can be a shame to bring a fine double-barrel into the rough and tumble world of duck hunting. Somehow, it just makes sense to let an autoloader's stock get nicked up and its parts exposed to the salt, sand, and harsh elements of winter.

The semi-auto is a better choice for practical reasons. Most semi-autos and pumps are typically less expensive than double guns and are designed for duck hunting. They often feature synthetic stocks and weather-resistant coatings on the metal parts.

Finally, repeating shotguns are required to be plugged for three shots. This extra capacity can be helpful when the birds are flying fast and hard. That extra shell can be handy for downing a cripple or taking down that unexpected teal speeding over the decoys.

There is a variety of quality shotguns tailor-made for waterfowl hunting. Select one that can stand up to the type of duck hunting you want to do.

A suitable duck gun must be able to put up with the rigors of waterfowl hunting.

95

Mastering hunting camp duck poppers

DUCK POPPERS ARE TRADITIONAL HUNTING CAMP HORS d'oeuvres. Every duck hunter should know how to prepare them. This recipe was passed on to me by a friend and duck hunting mentor, Bob Murphy. Bob passed away a few years ago, but his spirit is felt every time we sit in the duck blind. There are many variations on the recipe: Some chefs add cream cheese or watercress. I like the simple duck poppers best. Feel free to add your own unique twist to this traditional duck camp recipe.

Duck poppers are simple and delicious hors d'oeuvres.

Ingredients:

4 medium-sized duck breasts

1 small jar of sliced jalapeño peppers

1 bottle teriyaki marinade/sauce

1 cup orange juice

1 package sliced, uncooked bacon

1 box of toothpicks (soaked in water overnight)

Directions:

Cut the duck breasts into bite-sized pieces. Remove any shot left in the meat. Mix the orange juice and the teriyaki sauce to make the marinade. Add the chunks of duck breast to the marinade and put them in a container or ziplock bag. Refrigerate for three to four hours or overnight, if you prefer.

To prepare the poppers for the grill, take one cube of duck from the marinade along with a slice of jalapeño pepper and then wrap it in bacon. Hold it all together with a toothpick. Soak the toothpicks in water overnight to prevent them from burning on the grill. Cook until the bacon is done. Inside, the duck should come out a prefect rare to medium rare. Enjoy!

PART

XII

Final Thoughts

96

Study the classics on shooting technique

THE CRAFT OF SHOOTING A SHOTGUN HAS BEEN STUDIED for centuries. Throughout the shotgun's history, there have been many who have mastered the art of teaching shooting. I love this subject, and there are many classic titles any shooter should have in his library. The more you know about the fundamentals of shotgun shooting, the better shot you will become.

The forefathers of shotgun-shooting technique are Percy Stanbury and Robert Churchill. These men taught and honed their craft in England: Robert Churchill was an instructor and a gun maker, and Percy Stanbury taught out of the famous West London Shooting School.

Robert Churchill's book *Game Shooting* is considered to be one of the definitive books on instinctive wingshooting. Percy Stanbury's book *Shotgun Marksmanship* is the foundation for modern clay shooting techniques. His book and teachings also influenced game shooting worldwide. Each of these men had his own unique style and theories on shooting game. Interestingly, they were very different in terms of size and stature. Stanbury was long and lean in his body type, and Churchill was a bit shorter and had a thicker build. They taught slightly different techniques, most likely influenced by their own body types. Differences in technique can be clearly seen in their footwork and stance.

Other titles to consider are *Gunfitting* by Michael Yardly, *Shotgunning* by Bob Brister, and *The Orvis Wingshooting Handbook* by Bruce Bowlen. I've had the pleasure of teaching and working with Bruce over the years. He is a fine writer and instructor, and his book neatly explains the finer nuances of wingshooting.

Other books by Michael McIntosh on shotguns and shooting are interesting to read and contain a vast amount of useful information.

Take time to study these classics and other books on the subject of shotgunning and wingshooting. It will make you become a better and more knowledgeable shooter.

Study the classic books on wingshooting. They can improve your technique and make you a more well-rounded shooter.

97

Shooting in the zone— develop a pre-shot routine

A pre-shot routine can give you a competitive edge.

HAVE YOU EVER HAD ONE OF THOSE DAYS WHEN THE BIRDS just seem to fall every time you rose up and pulled the trigger? Did you ever run ten straight on a sporting clays stand? It's as if you just knew the clay was going to bust even before you pulled the trigger. Most likely, your mind was absent of thought and your eyes were locked in on the clay. The body's reaction was smooth and effortless in its connection to the target.

This is what we call "shooting in the zone." Whenever I'm coaching a student who's on a run, I just watch. I can clearly see that the shooter is blocking out the world around him and is calmly reacting to the target with confidence. After the shooter is finished shooting, I will ask him what he was thinking while he was busting all those clays.

Often, the shooter will give me a puzzled look, as if he were unable to remember what just happened or what he was thinking.

The "zone" is a mental state in which the eyes lock in on the target and the body reacts in perfect harmony with the target. The mind becomes clear and uncluttered. The eyes remain focused on the target. The body and mind work seamlessly together in a smooth, positive reaction to the bird in flight.

The zone is the ideal mental state for optimum performance. Your mental outlook and thoughts can have a great deal of influence on your shooting performance. For example, if you step up to a target and think, "This looks hard. Man, is this clay crossing fast. I'm never going to be able to hit this," chances are, you will have a very hard time busting that target. Negative thoughts often create negative results. If you can't envision breaking the target, you are not setting yourself up for success.

The body seems to follow the mind's direction. If you can see yourself busting the target out of the sky, the mind can help influence the body to do so. This may not work every time, but negative thoughts do work almost 100 percent of the time.

The first step in finding your shooting zone is to develop a consistent and repeatable set of fundamentals. Once your body masters the swing and gun mount, you are ready to shoot in the zone. Remember, the zone is about having a clear mind, reacting without thought. If you have to think about how to mount the gun, focus is taken away from the target. The only real difference between an expert and a beginner is that an expert has mastered the fundamentals. Master the fundamentals, and it will become easier to consistently shoot in the zone.

The best way to put yourself in the zone is to develop a pre-shot routine. A pre-shot routine sets you up for success. Pre-shot routines can be somewhat elaborate or very simple. Most world-class shooters use the loading process, or closing of the gun, as kind of a switch. When they close the gun, they rehearse moving the gun to the break point as they picture the clay exploding. Others might say "Focus!" or "Detail!" in their head before calling for the bird. This forces them to concentrate and look for something specific on the target.

The goal of a pre-shot routine is to remove any doubt or negative thoughts and switch the shooter's focus onto the target.

Even wingshooters can have a pre-shot routine. Once the dog goes on point, you can employ a word or ritual that draws your attention to the task at hand. I have hunting buddies who use key words when they are on alert for a flush. This even works over flushing dogs. Whenever a flushing dog gets a "birdy," you can have a quick pre-shot routine or word that goes off in your head.

For example, when I'm duck hunting, sometimes I say "picture" as I'm flipping off the safety. This makes me focus on some detail of the duck. This little phrase allows me to picture the lead or makes me focus on the bill of the duck. Anything you can do to sharpen your focus before taking the shot will improve your performance dramatically.

98

The mental game— shooting psychology

THE HUMAN MIND IS AMAZINGLY EFFICIENT. IT OFTEN DOES exactly what we have programmed it to do. Even if the outcome is undesirable, sometimes it is our own thoughts that have put the wheels in motion to produce these unwanted results.

It works like this: A client will come to the shooting school and state right off the bat: "I'm not a natural shot. I just can't seem to shoot consistently. I don't think I'll ever be a good shot." It's really fascinating because almost everyone who comes to a school with these thoughts starts out as a poor shooter. Even when they have wonderful hand-eye coordination, they still end up shooting far below their ability. Why? Because they have programmed their subconscious to believe that they are below-average shooters.

The mental game of shooting can greatly influence your performance.

Sounds crazy? Not to Dr. Bob Rotella, a leader in the field of sports psychology, who works with many of the world's top professional golfers. Rotella says that the subconscious mind and our self-image can have a tremendous effect on our performance. According to Dr. Rotella, if you continually feed the subconscious negative thoughts about your shooting, your self-image as a shooter will be formed in a negative way. Even though your conscious mind would like you to be a wonderful shot, you will subconsciously try to fulfill the negative self-image you have created in your mind. So in essence, if you say you are a poor shot often enough, your subconscious will try to make you a poor shot.

I see this all the time with students who tell me that they are never going to be good shooters. They will break several difficult targets in a row, and then seemingly out of nowhere, they will begin to miss targets. Then, the struggle begins. This often has nothing to do with hand–eye coordination, age, or experience. I believe they have all the skills needed to break even the hardest of targets, but their self-image as a shooter is holding them back. They have programmed their subconscious to make them inconsistent shooters.

The metal game of shooting can be very specific. Overall, you might consider yourself an excellent clay shooter, but you may think that you are terrible on left-to-right crossing shots. Again, I see this all the time. The shooter who states that he is terrible at a certain target presentation often is deficient at this shot compared to the rest of his shooting ability. Sometimes, he needs an adjustment in shooting technique, but often it's just his thinking that created poor performance on that shot.

The mental game is very important when it comes to overall shooting performance. Learn from leading sports psychologists to understand how to change your thinking. Begin programming your subconscious with positive thoughts and avoid negative thinking. This will make you a better and more consistent shotgun shooter.

99

Practice makes permanent

DO YOU REMEMBER THAT OLD SAYING "PRACTICE MAKES perfect"? Well, that's not exactly true. Actually, practice makes permanent. I first stumbled on this saying years ago, and it has stuck with me. I read it on a flight in a golf magazine. The author was Dave Pelz, who is a putting guru. The statement intrigued me. After reading it, I did a little digging. It turns out that practice can in fact make permanent, but not necessarily perfect.

What this means for the shooter is that you should ensure that your form is correct when practicing your shooting. A trained or experienced coach can help ensure that your fundamentals are correct.

Often, when coaching shooters during a private lesson, I will give them homework to do until our next lesson. I encourage them to have short, meaningful practices sessions. If they need work on gun mount, I might take a short video of them making the move with perfect form and encourage them to watch it before a short practice session at home. I tell them to mount the gun fifteen or twenty times the right way. This can often lead to rapid improvements in their fundamentals.

I subscribe to the adage "Perfect practice makes perfect," taken from the legendary football coach Vince Lombardi. This philosophy seems to hold true. Research shows that the way you practice can matter more than how much you practice. I always recommend short sessions when you first make sure that your form is correct.

Often during longer shooting sessions, the body begins to tire. This is when form begins to break down and bad habits can creep in. At the Orvis Shooting Schools, we have the student instructor ratio of 3 or 4 to 1. Each student gets plenty of shooting throughout the day. However, the students each receive many short training sessions throughout the day. This way, even during a full day of shooting, you can avoid having bad habits creep in due to fatigue.

Be sure that your practice sessions are productive. Think quality over quantity. Learn to practice and shoot with the correct fundamentals. This will improve your overall shooting performance and allow you to avoid the pitfalls of developing bad habits.

Practice makes permanent, not perfect. A trained set of eyes can ensure that you are building proper fundamentals.

100

You can never have enough fly rods—or shotguns

FLY RODS ARE MADE IN A VARIETY OF DIFFERENT WEIGHTS and lengths. Fishing for small-stream brook trout is vastly different from casting to tarpon off of the deck of a flats boat. Each of these fishing situations requires a suitable fly rod. The same concept applies to wingshooting. Hunting woodcock in the alders is vastly different from shooting geese in a layout blind in a muddy cornfield. For this reason, the type of shotgun best suited for each type of hunting situation can be vastly different.

In shotgunning, it's difficult to have one gun that is ideal for every shooting discipline. One can certainly get away with shooting a twelve gauge for most types of shooting or hunting. For some situations, you may have way too much gun, and on other days, you might need a tighter choke or heavier shot. However, there is really no single shotgun that is perfect for every shooting scenario.

This is why the serious shotgun enthusiast often has several shotguns. Each gun is suited for a different type of clay shooting or hunting situation. I have a small gun safe full of shotguns, including a sweet little twenty-eight-gauge for woodcock, grouse, and quail, and I have several twelve-gauge shotguns, one of which is an autoloader for duck hunting. I also have an over-under for sporting clays, and sometimes I take it pheasant hunting. I've got a twenty-gauge autoloader that my wife uses. It has very little recoil for clay shooting, and it's a serviceable duck gun over decoys.

I recently acquired an over-under twenty-gauge. I bought it mostly because it fit me, and I liked the look of the gun. Right now, I'm in the market for a .410 for my son to practice with.

You can never have enough fly rods or shotguns. Filling up a gun safe can make for some good fun and may lead to some fond memories.

There is no one ideal gun for every shooting or hunting situation. That's why passionate shooters always seem to be in the market for another shotgun.

Focus—again!

THERE ARE MANY TIPS THAT HAD TO BE LEFT ON THE cutting-room floor, so why repeat a tip on focus? Because focus is so vital to the shotgunner.

I have had the privilege of working at the Orvis Shooting School for almost twenty years. Bird hunting and clay shooting are both enjoyable, challenging pursuits. I have been fortunate to have hunted in some of the most wonderful places that game birds roam. I've also had the opportunity to bust my share of clay targets.

I've taught some 10,000 people the art of shooting a shotgun. The single most important tip that I have seen helps our shooters is focus.

What do I mean by focus? It means to lock your eyes in on the clay or bird you are shooting at and block out everything else. You don't have to have 20/10 vision to look for some detail on the clay. Focus means to clear the mind of clutter and look for some detail on the bird.

The fundamentals of shooting are very important if you want to shoot at your very best. Above all else, however, you must be able to block out any distraction and look only at the target as it flies through the air.

You could have a perfectly fitted gun, the best gun mount, and the best footwork, but all of that will do you no good if you can't focus your full attention on the target. The ability to pick up and lock in on the target trumps all. The gun will simply not shoot where you want it to if you don't have your eyes focused on the target.

Unfortunately, the psychology of a miss makes focusing on the bird counterintuitive. When we blank on a target, we are often asking ourselves, "Where did I miss?" On the very next shot, we are tempted to look down the rib to see where the gun is lining up with the bird. This is the worst thing to do when you are missing targets. After a miss, you need to look more intensely at the bird. Instead of seeing the clay flying through the trees with a nice, blue sky behind it, you must look at the leading edge of the clay. This narrows your focus and puts your shot pattern on the bird.

Remember, when you just can't seem to hit a target, switch your focus to the bird, and you'll be back in the game in no time.

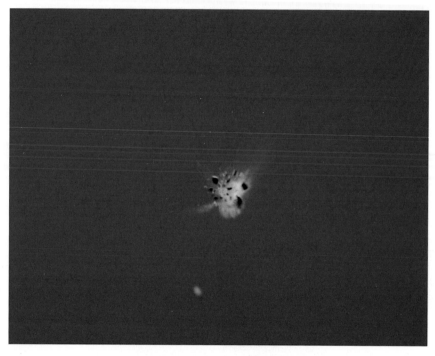

Focus, or visual concentration, can often be the difference between a miss and hit!

Acknowledgments

THERE ARE SO MANY PEOPLE TO THANK WHOSE HELP AND support made this book possible.

A special thanks to Greg Cutler. Thank you to James Ross, Brian Long, and to everyone at Orvis Sandanona. Thank you to Bruce Bowlen, Truel Myers, and all the instructors at the Orvis Wingshooting Schools. Thanks to Jordan Smith and his fine dogs. Thank you to Lars Lacob. A special thanks to John Rano for all our wonderful days afield.

Thank you to my editor Jay Cassell. Jay, thanks for putting up with me on another book.

Lastly, and most importantly, I must thank my wonderful wife Deborah Henley. Debbie, thank you so much for allowing me to follow my dreams and for supporting me in everything that I do.